THE GREAT DEBATE

Books by Glenn Slade Clark, Jr.

Novels and Collections

Cry, Wolf

The Great Debate

Metrognomes: The Shaman's Apprentice

Short Fiction E-Books

The Rainbow-Colored Sheep

The Ghost in the Olive Grove

Aries' Cage

Ooga Booga Stories:
Night Light
Night Light II

Metrognomes:
Music of the Metrognomes
Worse than a Gremlin

Dr. Coffee's Pill

Breath

Hollow Jane

The Escapist

The Gift

The Legends of Nod

The Briar Patch Evangelist

Benches

Serial Fiction E-Books

The Chronicles of Nightfire, Texas 1-13

THE GREAT DEBATE

Glenn Slade Clark, Jr.

CLARK
INK
LLC

2012

The Great Debate

"The Rainbow-Colored Sheep" was originally published in 1999.

Cover art by Molly Brimer.

Illustrations by Valerie Clark ("The Rainbow-Colored Sheep" and "Reverend Philips is Going to Hell") and Molly Brimer ("Six Nights to Damnation" and "Christian's Dilemma").

ISBN-10: 1-61815-036-7
ISBN-13: 978-1-61815-036-3

Dedicated to Charlotte Deaton,
for lending me her courage,
when mine was not enough.

CONTENTS

▼

THE RAINBOW-COLORED SHEEP

"So when they had dined, Jesus said to Simon Peter, 'Simon, son of Jonas, do you love me more than these?'

"Peter said to him, 'Yes, Lord; you know that I love you.'

"Jesus said to him, 'Feed my lambs.'

"Jesus said to him again, the second time, 'Simon, son of Jonas, do you love me?'

"Peter said to him, "Yes, Lord; you know I love you.'

"Jesus said to him, "Feed my sheep.'

"Jesus said to him the third time, 'Simon, son of Jonas, do you love me?'

"Peter was grieved, because Jesus said to him the third time, 'Do you love me?' and he said to him, 'Lord, you know all things; you know I love you.'

"Jesus said to him, 'Feed my sheep.'"

—John 21:15-17

It happened one day that the master rose and said to his shepherd that he would be leaving, for a time, but would soon return. The master was gentle and kind, and he loved us all—the sheep of his flock. He loved us, and he knew us in each and every aspect of our individual ways. He had raised a multi-colored flock.

Before the master left, he said to his shepherd, "Feed my lambs. Watch over my sheep." He handed the shepherd a book of instructions for our care, and then he went away. He had business with his father, who lived in a kingdom far, far away.

Times were trying in those early days, just after the master's departure. The wolves were ravenous, and they came out of the wilderness to harm us, but the shepherd kept the flock secure, and we managed to survive.

Now that the master has been gone for so long, my brothers concur that living as his sheep has surely grown easier. I turn my head, for I disagree, but I keep my thoughts within.

Though the master loved us all, the shepherd has grown insane and now tends only select members of the flock with the love we *all* once knew. The flock had once been so diverse, so beautiful and colorful, but the shepherd has changed that. I do not deny that, without the shepherd, the flock would not have lived at all in the master's absence. At the same time, however, I will not deny that the shepherd is a liar and a fiend.

The master has been gone far longer than any of us expected, and I know that the shepherd does not truly believe that he will return at all. That is why the shepherd has no fear to twist the instructions in the master's book. He has no fear when he wishes to impose his own twisted will upon the flock—even against the master's loving nature.

The master picked us all by hand—a multi-colored flock. This makes it impossible for me to understand what has happened—what the shepherd says is written in the master's time-scarred book.

He tells us now that the master wrote to only feed the white-woolen sheep. When the master returns, only the sheep with pure-white wool may follow him to his father's kingdom. How can this be! How can the master pick us all by hand and love us every one, only to forsake any he picked that were not white!

Now it seems the shepherd has his way. All the flock is white now—waiting on the master's alleged return. All the flock, that is, save me—the rainbow-colored sheep.

I love my brothers. I cannot leave, even though I know that I am not welcome anymore. The master loved me. This I know, though the shepherd does not tell me so. His words are harsh and unkind to me. He has turned my brothers against me with his lies and fearless prejudice. While some will gladly speak their mind, most of my brothers treat me well when the shepherd is not standing over them, but even so he has tainted their thoughts. I know what they think; that I do not belong. I hear them talk when they think I cannot hear.

I love my brothers! I love them more than words can say! But they fear me now, for the shepherd's lies! It is no longer right for them to love me. Why can they not just love me! I know that my fleece is not considered appropriate for the flock, but I am not asking them to trade in their own white fleece for a coat as colored as mine. I ask them only to love me for who I am beyond my wool.

My coat does not define me. I think and love the same as they do. And I do not believe that just because my fleece is not white, I am not a good sheep too. I do not believe what the shepherd says; that the master is not pleased with me; that the master will not have me. If that were true, then why would I even be here to begin with? Was it not the master himself who added me to his flock in the beginning?

The other colored sheep are lost. When the shepherd stopped feeding them, they fled into the forest. The wolves are in the forest, but they feel the risk is worth it to escape the hurt of staying with the flock. Even though they love their white brothers still, they could not bear to live in a place devoid of both love and nourishment for themselves. The wolves may kill them, and I worry to the core of my soul, but at least they feel community with each other. They have no shepherd to care for them, but at least they have among themselves love and acceptance — though I know they miss the flock, and I know the flock misses them, but these are matters forbidden to discussion.

I often wonder about the master's return. Will he go into the forest himself and rescue my colored brothers? Or will he look at me crossly and send me to join them?

Will he return at all?

Day by day I waste away. The shepherd will not feed me. The flock will not defend me. My colored brothers in the woods do not know why I stay. The white sheep of the flock do not know why I refuse to hide myself in flour or chalk. It offends them that I choose to stay *and* let my colors shine.

I alone know why I stay, and I alone am suffering. I stay because I love the flock. I stay because I fear the wolves.

Tonight I sleep alone beneath a tree that has no leaves. The rain comes down and soaks my rainbow-colored wool. My only comfort is in the fact that the rain-drops hide my tears. The shepherd has taken my brothers beneath a tree that has so many leaves. They cannot feel the rain at all, but they had no room for me.

My pain is unbearable. My tears are unending. I am all alone, so wet and cold. My body is starving and so is my soul. I miss my brothers in the woods. They scold me for not joining them, for they so detest the shepherd and his book. I am tempted by them. I *could* leave, but I could never be happy because of it. It is just as well that I am unhappy where I already am.

I miss the love and approval of my brothers in the flock. They tempt me just as well. I *could* cover myself in white flour, but I could never be happy because of it. It is just as well that I am unhappy with the colors I already have.

This division has torn me, and I know that my master would never have approved. He loved me, I know, so why don't they?

It's almost a pity that I cannot hate anyone. If I could hate, then I could choose.

SIX NIGHTS TO DAMNATION

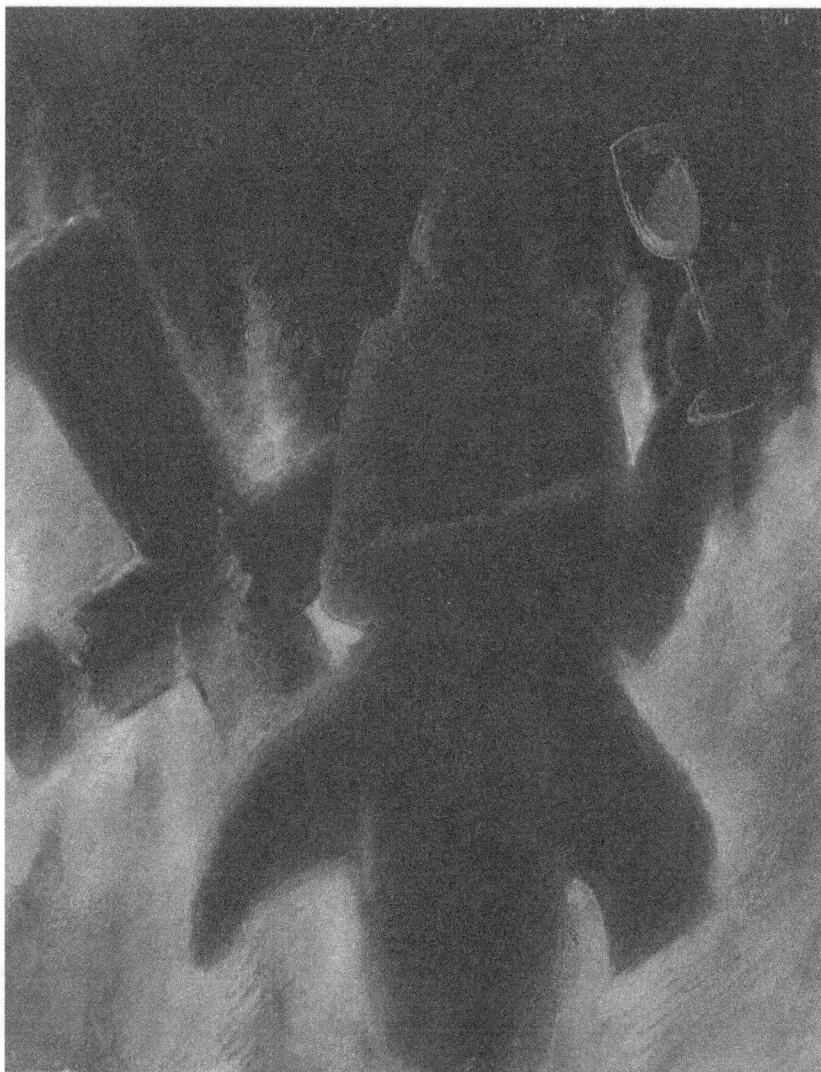

"The other colored sheep are lost. When the shepherd stopped feeding them, they fled into the forest. The wolves are in the forest..."

—The Rainbow-Colored Sheep

1

"That's them! They're here!" Fifty-year-old Betty Paul quickly rose from the small kitchen table, where she had been visiting with one of her nephews and an old family friend, to answer the front door. When she opened it, she gasped and found herself holding back tears at the sight before her.

A dark-haired, dark-eyed, young man smiled up at her brightly—just the way she remembered him smiling as a boy. "Hello, Aunt Betty. Sorry I'm late."

"Late!? Oh, Anthony, it's been four years! You look absolutely dashing! You don't look twenty-six at all. In fact, you don't look a day over twenty!" She practically leapt at him, which was no small feat for a woman of such vast weight, as she embraced him with a hug she'd been holding back for years.

As Anthony returned her hug, Betty glanced over his shoulder at his traveling companion. "And neither one of you looks old enough to be married." She smiled at the young woman behind them—a fiery red-head, if ever there was one. She broke the hug and addressed her, "You must be Eleanor! I feel as if I already know you! Anthony has spoken so eloquently of you in his letters, and with such detail. I dare say that you're even more beautiful than I had imagined."

Eleanor blushed slightly but did not turn from Betty's gaze. "Thank you..." She hesitated.

"Aunt Betty! You'll call me Aunt Betty, because that's who I am" She went forward and hugged Eleanor warmly. "Welcome to the family, Eleanor. It's so good to finally meet you in person." She broke the hug and looked sharply in Anthony's direction. "Two months! You've been married nearly two months, and I'm only just now meeting her!" She shook her finger at him, and he grinned.

"Sorry, Aunt Betty, but we had the honeymoon and all, and you know how that goes."

"Not for two months, you didn't."

"Well, you know that I've been busy moving, now that I've left the newspaper in Nightfire and taken that teaching job in Denver. But why dwell on time lost? We're here now, and it's so good to see you again." He smiled affectionately at the woman who had raised him from the age of eight.

She looked sadly into his dark eyes. "Yes, but for how long? You'll leave for Colorado again in less than two weeks to start your new job." She put her hand on his face, "Oh, Anthony, why must you always stay so far away from home?"

Anthony smiled wanly—lost to any answer for her question. Eleanor stood uncomfortably beside him, not knowing quite what to say to this talkative stranger.

The silence proved too much for Aunt Betty, and excitement lit her rosy cheeks once more. "Let's go inside. I'm not the only one who's been missing you these four years! Bring your bags and follow me to the kitchen." She turned and went into the big, old house. Anthony and Eleanor exchanged amused glances as they followed her inside.

As the two newly-weds followed Aunt Betty through the entryway and towards the kitchen, she continued to gab. "I'm afraid you just missed your cousin Trixie. She left only an hour ago to go on a cruise with a man she met just two days ago. We see her only the slightest bit more frequently than we see you, and on this visit she did manage to give us all quite a shock, but I'll tell you about that a little bit later.

"Your cousin Benjamin is doing well. He just recently graduated from law school at the top of his class. I don't know what I'd have done if your Uncle John and Aunt Kate had left me that one to raise. I'd have fallen to a stroke by the time he was fifteen. He was always quite the lady killer, and still is from what I hear. It must be that blonde hair and those blue eyes of his.

"You could have done better even than Ben with the girls in your youth if you'd have wanted to of course, Anthony. I don't know why you never chased after the girls like he did, but I can see that holding back has served you well."

Anthony and Eleanor smiled at each other, as they followed hand in hand. "Don't worry, El," Anthony spoke purposefully loud enough to be heard by his jabbering aunt. "She has to take a breath sometime."

"I heard that," Aunt Betty said, as she finally entered the kitchen. She spoke to the guests she had left there moments before, "Get up, boys, and look at what I found on the front porch!"

Anthony and Eleanor entered the little kitchen, and just as soon Anthony dropped his bags and shouted with joy, "James! Derek!" He ran to hug them both. He first hugged James and then Derek, and then he introduced his wife, with his arms around both men. "Eleanor, this," he indicated the tall man to his right, "is my brother James. And this," he indicated the bulky man to his left, "is the friend who could easily pass as my brother, Derek Andrews." He left the two men and went to put his arms around his wife. "And gentlemen, this is my beautiful wife Eleanor."

Eleanor spoke first, "It's very good to finally meet you both." She held out her hand.

James offered his own hand and shook hers awkwardly. "Welcome to the family, Mrs. Paul."

Derek took her hand next and kissed her gently on the knuckles. "A privilege, Eleanor."

Eleanor studied the men who now stood before her. To see Anthony and James standing side by side, one could never have guessed that they were brothers. One could certainly never have guessed that Anthony was the elder by two years. While Anthony had brown eyes, a full head of thick, dark hair, and looked much younger than he actually was, James, who stood much taller than his older brother, had gray eyes, a head of light brown hair that was both thinning and receding, and looked much older than he actually was.

Derek was a tall and muscular man. He wore a cowboy hat, boots, jeans, and a blue, denim shirt. He did not look at all the sort to be so close to men with the looks of Anthony and his brother. His rugged features were as far removed from their fair and polished looks as was black removed from white and day removed from night. Still, there he stood beside them, the man who had so often been mistaken for the third Paul brother in the days of their youth.

"Well, aren't you both charming?" Eleanor said with almost giddy approval.

Derek shook his head. "Nope." He looked over at Anthony. "'Bout time you got back down to Houston, son! Hell, I haven't seen you for more than two weeks in the past eight years! I wasn't able to stop by much during the summer between your college graduation and the newspaper job. Now you're only gonna be in town for a few days before you're off again, and I may not get to see you again 'till sometime next week, prob'ly *right* before you and the little lady pack up and go.

Anthony put his hand on his friend's shoulder. "Then we'll have to make the best of the time we've got. Tonight, all drinks are on me. We'll catch up so completely with each other that our conversation will seem to wake the sun."

"Hm." James said nothing more than this.

Anthony looked over at his brother, who seemed unusually quiet and uncomfortable. Derek spoke on James' behalf, "That sounds great, buddy. Unfortunately, I have to leave soon, because I've got to be on a plane to Arkansas first thing in the morning. And I'm afraid that the drinking would be just between the two of us, since the snob here doesn't touch the stuff 'cept for Communion."

A look of shock painted Anthony's face, as he was dragged back to the present. "That's right!" His smile lit the room, as he regarded James. "My brother has continued the family tradition and become a Catholic priest! How could that have slipped my mind?"

The Paul family had always had a strong, Christian tradition, and Anthony had always been proud of this. His own father had been a priest briefly, before meeting the woman of his dreams. Anthony thought of how proud their father would be of James, and he felt his own pride increase seventy times over.

"Why do you seem so surprised," James asked his brother. "My Ordination Ceremony slipped your mind too, if you'll remember."

Anthony held up his hands defensively. "Hey, that's not fair! You know I had to work."

"Wedding invitations also slipped your mind, son. What the hell was that all about?" Derek questioned him in mock-offense.

Anthony laughed to hide his guilt. While it was true that he had been working, Anthony knew that he could have arranged some time to visit during the past several years, if he had really wanted to. And as for the wedding, Eleanor was not one for crowds. She hated to be in any situation where she felt like she was on display. It had taken Anthony a full month and a half of endless, strategic convincing just to get her to agree to meet his beloved Aunt Betty. "Don't take it personally, guys! No one was invited." Anthony and Eleanor had planned their quiet, little wedding months in advance. "It was all spur of the moment. Just me, her, and a judge." Anthony lied to protect his new bride. He didn't want them to know that it had been she who had insisted on leaving them all out of the wedding.

Aunt Betty wrapped an arm around Eleanor possessively. "Well, Eleanor," she beamed, "what do you say we leave the boys to catch up?" Her smile broadened. "I've got so much to talk to you about." It was so rare that Betty found herself in the company of any female relatives, and her niece Trixie just didn't fit her ideal. Betty was now overly excited to have a nice, young, intelligent-looking niece-by-marriage to talk to about her dashing, young nephew. She even dared hope that Eleanor would actually be interested in seeing all of Anthony's baby Pictures and hearing all of the boyhood stories that Anthony had probably been too ashamed to tell her himself.

Anthony desperately wanted his new wife to know and love his aunt in the way that he did. He looked into Eleanor's nervous eyes and gave her a reassuring smile and a subtle nod.

Eleanor looked over at Betty and smiled. "That sounds like a fine idea."

Before the two women could even turn to leave the room, everyone's attention was taken by the clicking sound of running, unclipped paws. Anthony's anticipation had barely begun when it was answered by the entrance of a very old, raggedy-looking mutt. "Patches! Patches ol' buddy!" Anthony looked as though he were going to break down in tears, as he fell to his knees and grabbed the scruffy animal in an absolutely shameless hug. When in the presence of ever faithful Patches, Anthony was forever an eleven-year-old. He kissed the ancient canine square on the nose, and Patches jumped up and licked his face all over. He even managed the now scarce energy to wag his long, dirty tail as he did this.

Aunt Betty scolded the dog, "Patches, behave yourself. What are you doing downstairs?"

The dog looked over to Betty, then back to Anthony, whom he was still practically standing on, and he continued to wag his tail, as Anthony looked into his tired, old eyes.

Anthony exploded with lucid laughter. He leaned over and started running his hands all over the dog's head and back, scratching and playing. Patches, too, was as happy as he had ever been to be back in the company of his long lost playmate. "Patches! Oh, Patches, I've missed you so much! How can you still be alive! I'm so glad!"

At this point, a tear did escape from one of Anthony's joyful eyes. He sat still and studied his old, old friend. "I'm sorry." He leaned over and hugged Patches tenderly. "I didn't mean to stay away so long."

The other four adults in the room just looked at the tender reunion and smiled at each other. Aunt Betty found herself fighting back tears, but she and Patches had a long-standing agreement to pretend that they disliked one another, so she dared not let her softness show.

Anthony looked up, teary-eyed, and spoke to his lovely wife. "This is my dog." He smiled and laughed in disbelief. "This is Patches!" Still looking at Eleanor, Anthony spoke to the dog, "And Patches, this is my wife, Eleanor."

Eleanor looked around the room to find all eyes staring at her expectantly. She realized with quiet astonishment that everyone was waiting for her response to the introduction. *Am I actually supposed to talk to it?* She wondered.

Eleanor found herself feeling an incredible jealousy over the dog. In the past, Anthony had spoken about that dog with more affection than he had offered for any of his *actual* relatives. Eleanor knew that the bond between her husband and that dog was very tight—tighter than, she sometimes felt, was the bond between her husband and herself.

Anthony had rescued Patches from certain doom at the hands of some very mean-spirited thirteen-year-olds who had been whipping the dog with belts and pegging it with soda cans, early in the summer of 1980. Patches had been a two-month-old, nameless stray, and Anthony had been, at the time, an eleven-year-old with more mouth than muscle. He had returned home covered in mud and his own blood, most of which had come from his nose. He had two broken fingers and a black eye, but he had managed to get home with the puppy in his arms. Over the next seven years, Patches had accompanied Anthony everywhere the law allowed.

Eleanor calculated that the dog was now about fifteen years old, and she was disappointed that it was still alive. She hoped desperately that Anthony wouldn't want to take it with them to Colorado. Anthony could seem distant enough at times without competition. She smiled awkwardly at the creature who now held all of her husband's affections. "Hello, Patches." She squatted down beside them and scratched the old mutt on the head, "I've heard a lot about you, boy."

A tiny voice broke the moment, "Aunt Betty?"

All eyes suddenly turned towards the very young child who now stood in the kitchen doorway. Aunt Betty spoke with an embarrassed tone. She was not embarrassed that the child was out of bed, but rather she was embarrassed that she had not spoken of the child yet to Anthony and his wife. "Christopher. What is it, love? Why aren't you and Patches in bed?"

Anthony and Patches exchanged a look. Patches licked Anthony on the face and trotted over to the child, who instantly put a hand on his matted head.

"I'm thirsty," the boy said timidly.

At this point, it was Anthony and James who exchanged a look, and both broke into a quiet snicker. They remembered how they had used the same excuse to Aunt Betty, as children, when they were curious about the voices they heard her visiting with.

"I see," Aunt Betty said skeptically, as she eyed her two older nephews. "You and Patches get back to bed, and I'll bring you a little glass of water in just a moment. Go on now."

Christopher began to turn reluctantly, but then he paused and gazed up at Eleanor, wide-eyed. "Who are you," he asked.

"My name is Eleanor. What's your name?"

"Christopher Allen Paul."

"Well, it's very nice to meet you."

Christopher considered this. "You're pretty."

Eleanor blushed as Aunt Betty scolded the lad lightly. "Christopher. Go to bed now, sweetheart." Christopher turned with a sly grin and walked with Patches back towards his bedroom.

Anthony looked at his wife with amusement as he stood. "Well, well. Looks like I've got some competition." He looked to Aunt Betty. "Who was that?"

A mildly disgusted look came over Betty as she answered him, "That was your cousin once removed Christopher Paul. Didn't I tell you that your cousin Trixie had shown up with quite a surprise? Well, that's it."

A sad, caring look replaced her disgust as she continued, "I don't even know who his father is. I don't know anything about him, except that he's six years old and needs his Aunt Betty. Trixie just showed up here with him, and when she left, just as suddenly with that man, she just told me that there wasn't enough room on the boat for Christopher. I know what she really meant."

Anthony knew too. All too well. Another member of the Paul family was going to be raised by Aunt Betty. With Patches. The nostalgia came in full force with that thought, and he was filled with a thousand emotions all at once. Everything from the feeling of greatest kinship with the boy, to even the slightest twinge of territorial jealousy.

Aunt Betty's mood changed yet again, as she angrily considered her amoral niece. "That's what your Aunt Amanda gets for naming the girl Trixie in the first place! She practically instructed her to grow up that way! Do you know this makes two generations in a row to be born out of wedlock! First Trixie, and now Trixie's own son! I honestly hope she doesn't come back for him. Do you know that? If I'd had Trixie all to myself she'd be a much happier woman today. Even stable. I want to save that branch of the family. I will make an honest man out of Christopher! Besides, she won't be back for him. She's too much like her mother. At least Trixie had an interested father to run to every once in a while. Oh well."

"I'm surprised to hear he's Trixie's, actually," Anthony said with a grin.

Aunt Betty looked genuinely perplexed. "Why's that?"

"The way he was ogling my wife I could have sworn he was Ben's."

Aunt Betty rolled her eyes in mock disgust, and the men all burst into laughter. Eleanor just stood against a wall looking uncomfortable.

As if taking this for a cue, Aunt Betty took her stunning, new niece-by-marriage by the hand. "Come with me, Eleanor. We'll get Christopher a paper cup of water from the bathroom, and then I can fill you in on Anthony's childhood and teenaged embarrassments." She glared at Anthony pseudo-threateningly.

Anthony offered his bride a reassuring nod.

"Okay," Eleanor spoke rather timidly.

"We'll leave the men to their loud and obnoxious blathering and scratching. The sooner they get it all out of their systems the better. Trust me on that one. It's a zoo here when they all get together." Aunt Betty could still be heard echoing herself as she walked with Eleanor down the hallway and towards the hall bathroom, "A zoo!"

The three men laughed loudly, because they knew it was true.

*　　*　　*　　*

After half filling a small, paper cup with water, Aunt Betty led Eleanor upstairs to Christopher's room. "You know," she whispered to Eleanor, "this used to be Anthony and James' room when they were small. Then, after we remodeled, when Anthony was between eighth and ninth grade, it was just James' room."

26

The door creaked very quietly as Betty opened it, and they found both Christopher and Patches sound asleep when they entered. Betty smiled beside Eleanor as they stood before the bed. She shook her head as she walked over to turn out the lamp.

"You know," she said, as she led Eleanor back out of the room, "James used to be the same way. He and Anthony would always come downstairs for a Dixie Cup full of water whenever they heard me with company. I would send them upstairs, and James would instantly fall asleep as he waited."

"What about Anthony," Eleanor asked.

A troubled look flashed over Aunt Betty just before she spoke with a well-trained smile, "Anthony never slept easily as a child. I don't think he's even slept well since. No matter what, he would always have the most horrible nightmares. I honestly don't know what caused them. I know the easy answer would be to say they were caused by the trauma of his parents' deaths. They were such good people. But, he had this problem with nightmares even before then. All his life. I think his parents' drowning in that church van only made it worse."

"Drowning?" Eleanor looked very puzzled. "What do you mean?"

"Yes, dear. You can't mean that Anthony never told you how they died!"

"If they drowned, then no. He didn't. He told me only that they had been in a car accident. He never elaborated past that. He's not much for speaking of his parents, actually. I'd almost think he wanted to forget them."

Aunt Betty led Eleanor into a small library just across from Christopher's room, and she closed the door behind them. "Wanting to forget and not wanting to remember are often two very different things. Sometimes we try to forget things because they are horrible. Other times, we don't want to remember things, because they were too wonderful, and remembering causes us to realize their absence."

Eleanor nodded. She was amazed at her own calmness. Normally, when she learned that Anthony had kept something from her, she would be lost in a state of panic. *Why didn't he tell me? I'm not good enough for him! I'm going to lose him!* But there was something about Aunt Betty. Something that made her feel completely secure.

Eleanor did feel jealousy over everyone else she had met. She knew that it was cowardly and selfish to want to be the only person in her husband's life, but she could not deny how she felt.

She could never be Anthony's brother, who grew up with him and knew his every boyhood secret. She could never be one of the guys, sitting downstairs with Anthony, drinking beer and telling horribly tasteless jokes. She could never be her husband's loyal dog, whom he revered in his youthful memories above all family and friends. She could never be that small boy Christopher, with whom Anthony could so easily relate. Eleanor had to admit to herself that all of these realizations had filled her initially with panic, but there was just something about Aunt Betty. Maybe it was that none of the thoughts that so rattled Eleanor herself even fazed Aunt Betty. She just seemed so comfortable with everything. It was as though Betty's confidence in Anthony's love had become Eleanor's own, if only just in Betty's presence.

"How did Anthony's parents die... really?"

Betty went over to one of the many oak bookshelves that covered the four walls of the room— floor to ceiling. She removed a box from its dusty resting place and started to carry it over to the desk which, accompanied only by a single chair, was the only piece of furniture in the room. She then paused, changing her mind, and set the box down on the floor, along with herself. "Sit down, Eleanor dear." She patted the floor beside her, and Eleanor sat reluctantly across from her. Betty then opened the box, revealing a vast collection of photographs. Eleanor looked back to the shelf from which it had been taken, and she noticed, with a mixture of dread and excitement, that there were at least fifteen more boxes of equal size and larger.

Betty shuffled through the mountains of memories until she found what she had been seeking. "Here we are." She handed the old photo to Eleanor.

Eleanor studied it closely. She recognized the boyhood images of both Anthony and James. She was amused to note that Anthony was actually taller than his younger brother back then, and James had a full head of unruly, almost blonde curls. They were standing directly in front of two smiling, forty-something people that she did not recognize at all. She knew that they must be Anthony's parents. She flipped the picture over and saw, written there on the back: March 5, 1977. She giggled. "He was so skinny!"

Betty chuckled as well. "Yes. He was only eight then. That picture was taken just three days before they died." The smile fell from Betty's face. "You see, Martin had been a priest for several years, but he had to give it up when he met Veronica. She stole his heart, and he wanted more than anything to marry her. And, as you know well, he did, and they had two wonderful sons.

"Martin didn't leave the church after he left the priesthood, however. In fact, he probably became more involved. He and Veronica both took a very special interest in youth ministry. They went along with the church's youth choir tours and camp trips in the summer. They helped to run the very large youth group, under the direction of the church's youth director, of course.

"It was on one of these trips, early in the spring of 1977, that we lost them. See, the church had recently gotten a new youth director. He was a drunk. He normally hid it very well, but on that particular day it didn't matter. He drove the van, filled with youth, right off of a very small ledge, and they landed in a river, after flipping over at least once. Some of the youth had been knocked unconscious, and so had their new director at the wheel.

"I never did learn all the details, but there was a group of Boy Scouts along the river bank, conveniently enough, and they were remarkably prepared. The current was quickly pulling the floating van towards a very treacherous water-fall. The Boy Scouts somehow managed to tie a few rafts to the trees with some very long ropes. God knows what they'd been up to before. Anyway, some of them went out on the rubber rafts and got beside the van. Martin and Veronica got every one of those youth and even that drunken youth director off of the van before it went over. Neither one of them would leave until they had seen this done. Unfortunately, by the time they had finished unloading the director, the Boy Scouts' ropes ran out of slack, and they couldn't go any further as the current quickly sucked the swiftly sinking van towards the waterfall.

"Veronica tried to swim for the rafts at the very last minute, but the Current proved too strong for her, and Martin went over the fall in the van before he could do anything to save her." Betty smiled at her astonished young listener as tears began to fall from her eyes. "They died heroes. They went out with more virtue than anyone I have ever known before or since.

"The boys had been staying with me while their parents were away, and it was I who had to tell them what had happened. That was the hardest moment of my entire life."

A long silence followed.

"Anthony still has nightmares," Eleanor said finally. "Though, I don't think they ever have anything to do with his parents. I don't know.

Sometimes he wakes up screaming. Other times he just wakes with a terrified jerk. I've always been concerned about him because of it. If I may speak confidentially..."

Betty nodded understanding.

"...I think he may have lost his faith. Whenever he wakes from one of his nightmares, I always have to talk him down. He always wakes up convinced that he's completely damned."

*   *   *   *

The night carried on, without concept of time. Betty and Eleanor had long since gone to bed, and the men's conversation had long since gotten drunk.

"Are you fucking serious?" Derek was astounded at the words of his priest friend, as he slammed his beer bottle down on the small, round kitchen table.

"Derek, do you mind not using that kind of language?"

"Fuck yes I mind! Why the fuck should I talk like a fucking Muppet just because I'm in the presence of God's self-glorified, tight-assed messenger James Paul? I swear to God! Sometimes you say the most full of shit, ass-blown things, James! It's like the day you got that collar stuck around your neck you thought you became everybody's goddamned mother!"

Anthony spoke up in Derek's defense, "It was a pretty whacked out thing to say, James." He took a sip of his beer, as he waited for his brother to erupt. It was an old game, and it never failed to get out of hand.

James' high and mighty mannerisms never even faltered. "Well, I don't see how. Enlighten me. What did I say that was so wrong?"

Derek didn't give Anthony the chance to reply. "You said that Christopher is going to Hell, you fucking nimrod!"

"Nimrod was a mighty hunter before God. He was the founder of Nineveh, he united..."

"Suck my under-educated dick, bitch!"

Anthony found himself laughing out loud. It had been so long since he'd been witness to the antics of Derek and James. So long, that he had forgotten how angry James could make him at times.

James glared at his older brother. "I don't think that any of this is funny, Anthony. Unless you think Hell is a joke?"

Anthony put his bottle on the table as he rolled his eyes. "James, Christopher isn't going to Hell."

"He was born in sin. His name will not appear in the Book of Life."

Derek threw his hands up in exasperation. "I swear to God! He's not a Catholic, he's a fuckin' Puritan! You know, when he was off at Seminary, he was always arguing with his teachers! He's a raving nut! They gave him the top score on his final paper or whatever, just because it didn't make any sense! They didn't know what he was talking about, so they just assumed he was smarter than they were! I don't know how the Hell he keeps his job! Next thing you know, he's gonna be burnin' little, old ladies for witchcraft!"

"Derek, you don't know what you're talking about. You never even go to church. How long since your last confession? If you were to die tonight, I'd fear for your soul as well. You need to turn your life around. The way you live is evil."

"Evil? How do you figure, James? I do a lot of good! So what if I don't go to your fucking church on Sunday mornings! I do a lot of good! If God wants me to burn for all time because I don't tell you how many nuns I fuck each week, he can kiss my sacrilegious ass! I personally think that evil is a fucking lie! There is no such thing!"

"So. You're saying that Satan is not evil."

"No, dick-weed! I'm saying that Satan is a lie! A concoction of religion, intended to frighten people into submission! Do what the preacher says, or else you'll burn forever! Oh yeah, and by the way, God is love! That's stupid, James. It's stupid!"

Anthony finally managed to get a few words in, "Without evil, good is an empty word. Evil defines good."

"But who defines evil?" A mischievous smile appeared on Derek's face, as he realized that he had stumped both brothers. He decided to change the subject, before the great debate could resume. "So, Anthony, what ever happened to that novel you were supposed to write? I thought you were supposed to be rolling in dough by now."

Anthony looked down, away from Derek's gaze, as he offered a weak smile that hid his haunted soul. "I don't know. I'm workin' on it.

The table was suddenly quiet. Everyone had fallen deep into thought. After about twenty seconds, Derek could take no more. He looked at his watch. "Damn! It's after 3:30! I've gotta get outa' here. I've gotta catch a plane in less than four hours." He stood up and went to shake Anthony's hand.

Anthony took his friend's hand and stood to embrace him in a very tender, yet manly, hug. "Take care of yourself, Derek." He pulled back and smiled at the taller man. "I'll see you next week."

"Yeah! Damn straight! You better still be here, buddy!"

"I will. I'm not goin' anywhere."

Derek shook his head doubtfully as he went to the refrigerator and grabbed a beer for the road. "I've heard that before, son. Take care of yourself now." He looked over at James and lifted his bottle in the air as he walked out the door. "Take it easy, Father Bitch. See ya' next week."

When Derek had gone, Anthony returned to his seat at the table and slowly turned his near empty beer bottle around with his fingers, as he stared at it and pondered the multitude of things that had been brought to his mind during the night.

James yawned. "What about you, Anthony?"

Anthony looked up at his brother—surprised to be taken away from his thoughts. "Hm?"

"Do you believe in damnation, or do you think that it was all just contrived by the Church to frighten people into submission, as Derek so ignorantly insisted?"

Anthony considered that, as he continued to toy with his bottle. "I don't know." His mind drifted, as he pondered that thought. He knew that terrible things did happen in the world. He knew that supernatural things happened in the world, and that not all of them were even close to being holy. Anthony had been given a journal, written by one of his ancestors, that had belonged to his father. The journal mentioned horrible, demonic events from the middle of the last century that were so disturbing that Anthony had never shared the journal with any of his family members.

Anthony had also done a great deal of historical research on religions of the world. He had done enough research to know that no one denomination had all the answers. Anthony dared not tell his brother this, however. He knew that he would never hear the end of it. And he knew that his brother's accusation would be true: Anthony's faith was faltering. He hadn't lost his faith that there was *something* greater than the universe, but he could no longer say honestly that the Catholic Church had it all figured out. "I don't really know the meaning of damnation. If it happens at all, why? I honestly don't think that

God forsakes people for being born out of wedlock. It's not Christopher's fault. He had nothing
to do with it. All he did was come into the world.
I think his salvation will be based on how he
lives his life." *The same reason that I am surely
damned.*

Anthony automatically averted his thoughts
from this belief. "Christopher's a lucky boy." He
smiled at his brother. "Surely he won't turn out
any worse than the two of us. Aunt Betty will
keep him in line."

James was unmoved. "You and Eleanor should
have a second wedding ceremony."

"What? Why?"

"You said it was just you two and a judge. You
should be married in a church, by a priest. Your
marriage should be recognized by God."

"Oh, Christ!"

"Anthony!"

"Give me a damned break, James! What the
hell is up your ass tonight!" Anthony had
reached true annoyance at his self-righteous
brother.

"I'm only looking out for the people I care
about! I don't see why you have to all be so foul
to me!"

"James, you're jumping at shadows! I mean, if I looked at the world the way you do, I would probably just give up! What's the point?"

"Divine Judgment is not a shadow, Anthony. It's all that matters in the end!"

"Then why not wait 'till then to worry about it?"

"You have to prepare for it now. Judgment could come for us at any time. Neither of us knows when his time will come."

"Oh, just get off it for a while, will you?"

"Anthony, what if your time comes tonight? Are you ready for judgment?"

"Fuck me!" Anthony rose from his chair and left his bottle on the table. "You are nuts! You're obsessed with this, and it's really pissing me off!" He gathered his composure just barely enough to stop shouting. "I'm taking a walk."

Anthony stormed out of the house, and James sat in the kitchen alone, not at all sure whether or not he had been in the wrong for what he had said to his brother.

*　　*　　*　　*

Anthony was angry, and he was still being affected the slightest bit by all of the beer he had consumed, yet he was still clear-headed enough to find himself nostalgic over the familiar path he now found himself walking. But then, as Anthony had come to learn, nostalgia was one of alcohol's favorite tricks.

This was by no means the first time that Anthony had become angry over an argument with his brother and gone storming off in the middle of the night. Years ago, it had happened frequently. James would say something bull-headed and stupid, and Anthony would call Patches and storm out of the house. The only thing different about this instance, as far as Anthony knew, was that Patches had not come along. Patches was upstairs with Christopher, sleeping like a puppy.

Aunt Betty's house was located on the absolute last block of what Anthony had been taught was the decent part of Houston, Texas. Anthony now knew that things were not so black and white as he had been taught in his boyhood, but he still found himself deviously excited by the idea of wandering off, unprotected, beyond the mowed lawns and picket fences of Aunt Betty's neighborhood.

Several houses down the road, there were countless dirty stories unfolding, and there always had been, as far as Anthony knew. Just beyond all of the well-kept homes on Aunt Betty's street, there were several run-down convenience stores, catering to the needs of people whose virtues were equally as run-down. There was a pool hall that had once been a garage, from which Anthony would always hear the most frightening screams of men who refused to lose easily and women who refused to cooperate with their surely ungentlemanly expectations.

However, of all the things to be found in that area, that his Aunt Betty had deemed so unsavory, there was one thing that had always caused Anthony to tingle wickedly above all else. And as Anthony now approached this buzzing hive of filth and sin, it was this one thing that caught his notice, as ever before, to the extent of blocking out all that surrounded it. There was a bar across the street from him, second building to the right. This was a bar with no windows, and its outside appearance did all that it could to escape the notice of any non-interested parties passing by. Even so, it was no secret what that bar, boldly christened David and Jonathan's, was really all about.

Anthony let his thoughts drift back to his teens, as he walked on, and he thought about James. It had always been so easy for him to be the perfect male. It had always come so easily, and yet he had become a priest. Once again, James had succeeded with ease in an area that Anthony had trouble with. James was so certain in his faith, and he had always been so certain in everything else, whereas Anthony had not. That was probably why it never really took very much of James' high and mighty, thoughtless condemnation of anything to send Anthony into an absolute rage. Anthony realized that, subconsciously, he had first set out on this walk as a teen to spite his brother, though his brother had never known about it. It was the only way that Anthony could rebel against the brother to whom everything came so easily.

Anthony had sometimes almost hated his younger brother for that. Everything that had come, without effort, to James, was expected by everyone to come just as easily to Anthony. Anthony had always fought so hard to please everyone else. He had dated attractive girls, he had gone to church and pledged his allegiance to what he considered a warped denomination. He had played sports to prove his masculinity.

In the end, that was probably why he had moved to another city the moment an opportunity had presented itself. And he had stayed away. He had hoped that by moving away, he would not feel all the pressures he felt in Houston. He would have nothing to prove. Still, even so many miles away, he had wanted his family to be proud. Their possible disapproval had haunted him at every decision he had made. He had wanted to be the perfect man that they believed him to be. He had wanted to prove that he was just as good as James, if not better. He had married beautiful Eleanor.

Anthony loved Eleanor. He loved her very much, but it was still a constant battle that he fought within himself. It was very much an effort to be a lover for Eleanor. It was an effort that he had committed himself to for life, for better or for worse, in sickness and in health. It was too late to ever turn back, but Anthony detested that thought. He wanted never to think like that. He wanted to love Eleanor, and he had succeeded. He did love her.

Anthony was proud of himself, because it had been a considerably long time since he had last caught himself looking at another man. Anthony had been convinced that he was cured of that evil. Still, it was a shaky pride he felt, and it was based on a lie. He knew this very clearly, as he stood alone before the dull-painted door of David and Jonathan's.

Anthony's body was tingling with wicked curiosity. This was the most dangerous walk he had ever taken, as far as he was concerned. In his youth, he had always taken Patches with him. He knew he wouldn't go in if Patches was with him, because he couldn't take Patches inside, and he would never have left the loyal dog outside, unprotected. Now, Patches was at home. There was nothing to keep Anthony from actually walking through that door, just to see what it was like on the other side. No one would ever have to know.

Anthony had begun to quiver with anxiety, as he considered, one last time, the possibility of turning around and forgetting all about David and Jonathan's, just as he always had before. Ultimately, brushing the dark bangs out of his face as a final, neurotic act of procrastination, Anthony opened the door and stepped inside.

I don't fit in here. I don't belong here. They can smell my inexperience like a wolf smells meat. What am I doing here? Anthony fought his doubtful thoughts away and walked quickly over to the bar, where he sat down and tried to look natural.

The interior of David and Jonathan's was a far cry from the outside he had judged it by for so many years. In fact, it was hardly the terrible, sick place Anthony had imagined it to be. Aside from the lack of windows and the absence of women, it was really just another bar. Of course, the fact that it was still open also struck Anthony as odd. It was now almost four in the morning, and, as a result, the bar was nearly empty. The emptiness contributed greatly to Anthony's self-consciousness. He didn't like being so easy to spot. The only comforting thought he had was that no one he knew would ever know that he had done this.

The bartender approached Anthony. He was a young man, maybe a year younger than Anthony himself. "Hi." The man smiled brilliantly. "You're a new face. I'm Mike."

"Um, hi." Anthony's voice was shaky. He could sense that the bartender was attracted to him, and it made him endlessly nervous. He wanted the man to go away, but at the same time, he wanted him to stay. He spoke in a terrified tone, "I'm Anthony. Anthony Paul."

"Really." Mike leaned over on his elbows. "So, Anthony, are you single?"

Anthony looked into the bartender's bright, brown eyes, and he could not help but grin innocently. He thought about Eleanor and reminded himself that she would never know. "Yes. I'm very single."

Mike lit up. "You're lying!"

Anthony felt himself go pale. "Why do you say that?"

The bartender grinned flirtatiously, as he stood. "Because guys as beautiful as you are always taken. So, what can I get you? It has to be a soft drink, because it's after two. But I'm sure you knew that."

"Yes, well, I'll just have a Coke, then." Anthony could not hide the frightened exhilaration in his voice. This was the furthest he had ever taken this fantasy, and he was completely unsure of how far he would let it go.

"Sure thing, Anthony." The bartender spun around and went to prepare his customer's beverage, while singing along with the up-beat Erasure song that was playing on the speakers.

He came back instantly and placed a small glass of Coca-Cola Classic on the bar before Anthony, who laid some money down beside it. "Keep the change, Mike."

"Beautiful *and* generous! Keep it up, Anthony, and you'll be my favorite customer in no time."

Mike flashed his glowing, warm smile once again, as he spun off to deal with some old men at the other end of the bar.

Anthony looked sickly at the beverage he had ordered. His stomach was in too many knots for him to even consider ingesting it, but he didn't want to look weird. He turned around on his barstool to look at the people behind him. He noticed that there were televisions placed around the bar so that everyone could see. Unfortunately, at four in the morning, little was on that would keep anyone's interest. Anthony looked away from the televisions, and he had locked eyes with someone before he knew it.

Panic grabbed hold of Anthony so quickly, that he didn't even see the man smile at him. He didn't even notice whether or not the man had been attractive. He just spun back around in his seat and looked directly at the bar—hoping that he hadn't been noticed. He felt like a fool. *If I appear disinterested, he won't look back. What am I doing here? Oh, God, please don't let him talk to me!*

Anthony gasped suddenly, as he felt a hand on his shoulder. He turned around to see the pair of eyes that he had locked onto seconds before. He noticed that they were exceptionally beautiful, and they were accompanied by an equally lovely smile. The man himself was very tall; at least six and a half feet, and he was very lanky as well. Anthony found himself very flustered by the appearance of this beautiful stranger at his shoulder.

"Hello," the man said. "My name is Tobit. I saw you looking at me." Tobit offered his hand, and Anthony just stared at it, wondering what he should do. He studied the hand before him. The fingers were very long, and the nails were also long. They were not as long as a woman might keep them, but they were surely longer than a man generally did. Long nails on long fingers, this only added to the overall elegance of the man himself. There was not even the slightest hint of clumsiness about him, as one might expect from such a long, tall, meek-looking being.

"I...I wasn't...I mean..." Anthony half lifted his shaky right hand to meet Tobit's, but found himself unable to complete the gesture.

Tobit laughed quietly, as he leaned over to grab Anthony's cowardly hand, and he shook it powerfully. He sat down beside Anthony at the bar.

Anthony was blushing fiercely with the shame of his behavior—the knowledge of his own, shameful clumsiness and innocence in this situation. He looked away from Tobit's hypnotic gaze, and he studied the glass of Coca-Cola in front of him, as though it were the most interesting thing in the universe, in a vain attempt to hide the burning blush of his face.

Again, Tobit laughed knowingly. "Why are you so nervous? Surely you know that you are far more beautiful a man than I. Why should I intimidate you so?"

Anthony closed his eyes and took a deep breath. He then turned bravely to face Tobit, who rewarded him with a welcoming, seductive smile. He suddenly found himself allowing the situation to sink in. He was sitting in a gay bar, unknown to his wife, and he was about to let an absolutely mesmerizing stranger try his hand at his seduction. And what a hand this stranger held. Anthony reflected on his so far brief encounter with Tobit. He was amazed at the startling strength the man had displayed, while greeting him, with those long, elegant, frail-looking hands. And he had also been surprised by how cold they had felt to the touch. Tobit's voice was soft, yet commanding, and he spoke with such a strange accent. It was an accent that Anthony could not place, but Tobit carried it with such certainty and charisma.

Anthony studied Tobit's warm-looking smile, and he wondered if those lips were as cold to the touch as that hand had been. He managed an inviting smile of his own. "I'm...I'm not so...I don't know." He laughed at himself. "I'm just having such a weird day." He turned away, back to his untouched beverage. "And I'm not so sure that I agree with you, Tobit." His blush threatened to return at the mere utterance of the stranger's name, but Anthony pressed on boldly. "I've looked in the mirror a few times, and I just..." He looked back at Tobit. "I don't even begin to compare." Anthony's blush came in full force, but he did not turn away from Tobit. He knew that his attraction was already more than obvious.

Tobit delighted in the words of his newly made acquaintance. "You flatter me truly, with such clever words. I'm very glad that I didn't let you scare me off when you turned away from me so quickly." He Paused shortly before going on. "So, where's your dog tonight?"

"What?" Anthony found himself suddenly alarmed. "What do you mean?"

"Your dog," Tobit said, as though surprised that Anthony had questioned this. "Patches."

"How do you...Do I know you?"

Tobit laughed at Anthony's obvious alarm. "Don't worry. I just have a very good memory. Years ago, I would frequently see you walking your dog across the street. Whenever you grew tired of staring at this building, you would say to the creature, 'Come on, Patches,' and it would follow you home. I had always hoped that, some night, you would go walking without your loyal beast. I knew that you would come inside if you did. See? And I was right."

"You saw me then and still remember me so clearly? That was years ago. I've changed, and even so you couldn't have gotten a very good look at me!"

"True. I watched you from the shadows, and you never crossed the street. I considered many times approaching you, but you were much too beautiful. I was reluctant. Tonight is different, because you've come to me."

Anthony was momentarily nonplused. The man before him was such a puzzle. "That was a long time ago, and you don't look any older than nineteen, maybe twenty! If my guess were correct, you'd have only been about twelve when last I came near here. Now I'm curious, just how old are you?"

Tobit smiled, but it was a fake-looking smile. He looked away, then brightly back into Anthony's eyes. "How old are *you*? You surely don't look old enough for this place yourself."

"I'm twenty-six, and I know I look younger. It's a curse I've learned to live with."

"I'd say that such long-lasting youth is a blessing, in your case, Anthony."

"Now you." Anthony found that he had grown more comfortable, but he still quivered subtly with excitement. "How old are you, sir?"

Tobit seemed the slightest bit distraught, as he ran his long, pale fingers through his shiny, chin-length hair. He turned away, as though he did not know how to answer. Anthony took notice of Tobit's hair, as he did this. It was very clean and lustrous. It was mostly light brown, but it shimmered as the light caught the many strands of gold and red that were scattered throughout. The taller man finally answered, and there seemed a haunting glare to his eyes when he spoke, "As old as temptation."

Anthony rolled his eyes in humor at what he decided was Tobit's clever way of saying, "I'll never tell." He opened his mouth to speak, but was interrupted instantly by Tobit, who spoke excitedly after looking up to the digital clock on the wall behind the bar. "Anthony, I find you amazing, but I've got to go! Will you walk out with me?"

"Yes. Sure."

As Anthony stood to leave, Mike hustled over to say good-bye. He offered Anthony his hand, and then a firm shake. Anthony felt that the bartender was pressing something into his hand at the same instant. "Sweet dreams, Anthony," Mike said with that glowing smile. He released Anthony's hand, and Anthony found himself holding a small piece of paper. He looked down and saw a phone number written there. "Come back and see me some time!" Mike flashed his perfect teeth at Anthony once more before hurrying back to his work. Anthony smiled broadly. He wanted to laugh out loud, for he found himself exhilarated with the success of his wicked outing. He could barely restrain himself, as he walked out with Tobit.

When the pair had exited, they paused just outside the door. Tobit spoke, "How long will you be in town? I know you're just visiting, because you've been away for so long, you must not live here."

Anthony was again taken by surprise at how perceptive Tobit had proven to be. "I...I really don't know, to tell the truth. Several days, probably."

"Good. Will you meet me here again, tomorrow night, earlier than this? I want to know more about you! I haven't met someone so entirely lovely in...a very long time. Please, tell me that I'll see you tomorrow.

There was such calm command in Tobit's voice that Anthony could not have even begun to refuse. Besides, he had every intention of obliging his new friend. Anthony was perfectly entranced by this elegant stranger named Tobit. He found himself wanting to please him, wanting to listen to him, wanting to touch him. "Yes. I'll come back."

"Good. We'll talk then. We'll really get to know each other." Tobit again took Anthony's hand in his own cold, bony hand. "I will await our next meeting eagerly, Anthony. I'm sorry that I must rush off, but I have someplace to be before sunrise." He leaned down and kissed Anthony's knuckles lightly, and yes, Anthony noted, his lips were very cold, but the surge of exhilaration that was coursing through Anthony's body was anything but. "And your wife need never know." Tobit smiled as he released Anthony's hand, turned, and walked away.

Anthony was again puzzled, as he turned in the opposite direction and headed for home. Then he paused and looked at the ring on his finger. Tobit had once again proved frighteningly perceptive. Anthony didn't understand his own unquenchable curiosity, but he could not even bring himself to consider not returning on the following night. He simply *had* to know this

55

Tobit further! Anthony turned to look after Tobit, but found that the stranger had already vanished. As Anthony stood there, puzzling over how Tobit could have disappeared so quickly, he felt the little piece of paper that Mike had offered him, and as the wind picked up around him he relaxed his fingers, and he watched it fly away.

As Anthony walked up the walkway of his Aunt Betty's old house, he saw, to his amazement, that his brother James had waited for him the whole night. Anthony hung his head low when he reached the large, wooden porch. "James, I'm..."

"No. Don't do that, Anthony. I'm the one who needs to apologize. I'm sorry. I went too far. I hope you'll forgive me. I...I'm very happy for you and Eleanor. I really am. She's...she's very beautiful."

Anthony smiled up at his humble brother, and tears again filled his eyes as he considered the whole mess. He hugged his brother tightly, and James, reluctantly at first, hugged him back with equal ferocity. Anthony spoke as he held him, "Oh, James. How I've missed our little arguments."

The two brothers were still tightly embraced, as the sun peeked over the horizon.

2

"Anthony. Anthony, wake up!" Eleanor's voice slowly began to register, as it rang its alarm throughout Anthony's sluggish mind. He was dreaming, and he did not want to be disturbed. His sleeping mind had traveled to fantasies of Tobit and freedom, worlds of love and...vampires...monsters...Hell and Damnation...

Come to me tonight, Anthony...come to me and we will be together always...surrender your soul, and I will make you mine...I know you want to belong to me...

"What!" Anthony sprang up with a start. He lifted an arm and wiped the sweat from his brow, and he felt Eleanor's gentle touch, as she placed her loving arm around his shoulders. Thinking back on his nightmares, Anthony found himself intensely aroused. He looked into Eleanor's beautiful, emerald green eyes, and the feeling left him instantly. He looked away from her and tensed up completely at the lingering arm around his shoulders.

As if sensing this, Eleanor removed her arm and looked away from him. There was an awkward, silent moment, in which neither of them could explain the silence of the other. Then Eleanor spoke. "Another nightmare?"

"Yes."

"I have some bad news. Your aunt asked me not to wake you, but it's 9:30 at night. I was worried about you."

Shock suddenly painted Anthony's sweat-shined face. "What? 9:30?" He looked over at the clock by the bed. "Oh, crap! How did I do that?" A short laugh escaped his tense throat at the thought.

"Well, you did stay up pretty late last night." The couple at last locked eyes after she had said this. They were both looking for answers—she to see if he had them, and he to see if she had found them already.

"Well, I had a lot of catching up to do. I'm sorry." He made a pathetic attempt at a smile.

She again looked away from him, "You didn't even wake me when you came to bed."

"It was dawn. I didn't want to disturb you."

"You never seem to want to *disturb* me anymore."

"Eleanor, don't do this. You know that I love you. I've just been stressed out lately. Moving, changing jobs, catching up with friends and family after so many years. It just takes its toll. It's not you. It's me."

"I don't care, Anthony. I don't care! I don't want your excuses anymore. I want you to *do* something about it. Damn it. Just make an effort for me...if you think I'm even worth it."

Anthony turned away from her and put his feet on the floor somberly. "I...," he paused to find the words. "I'll make an effort for you, but I hate to say it like that. I hate to use the word effort. I love you so much." He turned and gazed into her eyes once again.

She looked down. "I know you think I'm just a bitch."

"Eleanor..."

"I have to tell you something," she interrupted him. "I just don't...I don't know what to say..."

Anthony stood up and adjusted his boxers, then he turned to look at her, greatly concerned. "What is it?"

She looked down at the sheets and said nothing.

"Eleanor, just tell me. I go mad when you do this. Please, just spit it out."

She looked up, tears in her eyes. "Your friend...Derek."

"What about him?"

"He's um...dead."

Anthony felt a sudden, Arctic chill. "What?" His eyes glazed over, and he felt paralyzed. The only way to keep from crumbling was to keep talking. "When? How? This isn't...this just can't be. Who told you that?"

"Your Aunt Betty found out this morning, at around eleven. She's been crying all day and looking through all of her photos. I think she must do that often...look through all those photos." She looked at her husband as he stood there, pale, his heart obviously breaking in two. Eleanor was hurting for him, but at the same time, she felt an incredible shame, for she was quite relieved to have Derek gone—never to monopolize her husband's time again. "Please don't hate me for telling you this."

"Eleanor, don't be ridiculous. You didn't kill him."

True, but she felt as though she had. "I wanted to wake you right away. I wanted you to know this when it happened, but Betty wouldn't let me. She wanted you to sleep peacefully at least once before hearing about your friend's death."

"She knows I never sleep peacefully."

"I know. She was just being optimistic. The funeral is Thursday morning."

"What happened? Was it the plane? Did it...?"

"No." Eleanor seemed truly disturbed by the words her mind was forming. "He, in fact, never even made it to his plane." She looked up, teary-eyed. "They found him in a dumpster, and...his throat had been ripped apart by something, or someone. I don't know. Nobody knows."

Anthony turned away from her completely. "Eleanor, I...need to be alone...for a little while."

No! Eleanor knew she was wrong to want him now. She knew that she had to be more understanding in this time of grief, but she could not help but feel panicked jealousy, even of the *no one* that Anthony would be with in his solitude. She stifled her feelings, for his sake, reason winning out over passion this time. "All right.

61

I'll tell Betty and James that you're up." As she walked out of the guest room, she spoke almost too hopefully, "And I'll be downstairs...if you should need anything." She closed the door behind her, and Anthony was left alone with his thoughts.

*   *   *   *

The shower was hot, but Anthony scarcely noticed it. As the steam surrounded him, and hot air filled his lungs, he thought only of Derek. How could this have happened? His throat ripped apart! Anthony felt the terrible pain of tears welling up, and he fought to hold them back, but the more he thought of his oldest and dearest friend, lying in a dumpster with his throat ripped out, the less was his strength to resist his sorrow. He broke into sobs, and he braced himself against the shower wall. "Why, God? Why?" He shook his head slowly, and without purpose. "Why? Why? Why? Oh, God, please don't let this be!"

Anthony wanted never to leave the shower. He wanted the moment in which he was never to end; for he felt that once he had stepped out of the shower, he would have accepted that he was living in a different world than the one he had last gone to sleep in. A world without Derek. Anthony suddenly hated himself for staying away so long. He hated himself for not being there when Derek had died. And he hated himself for being alive. He was filled with the irrational guilt of going on, when Derek could not. He felt as though he was betraying his friend by not being dead with him, by going on as though the world were no different without him. He felt as though going on was a slap in Derek's face, but he knew that Derek would want him to. He knew he was thinking emotionally and not rationally. Still, he did not want to leave the shower. To Anthony, the shower had become a bridge between two worlds. He had entered saying good-bye to one world, and he knew that he would leave it to greet the cold realities of another.

Anthony's thoughts drifted suddenly to Tobit. The fact that he had most likely been with the tall stranger when Derek had been ripped apart seemed somehow trivial next to the remembrance that he was supposed to meet Tobit again tonight, and he had slept until 9:30 P.M. Anthony was suddenly in a rush—having miraculously forgotten his pain, for the moment. He quickly finished with his shower, and he stepped out into that frightening, new world. It was a world in which Derek was dead, true, but it was also a world in which Tobit was waiting.

$$* \qquad * \qquad * \qquad *$$

When Anthony at last entered the small kitchen, he was far more polished than Eleanor had expected his grief to allow. He looked as though he were off to meet important people, rather than just emerging from his bedroom to meet his grief-stricken relatives in the kitchen. Eleanor was suddenly convinced that this was exactly what was going to happen. She felt a silent, jealous rage at whomever her husband was leaving to go see. She wanted to accuse him right then and there, but she knew far better. He hadn't even spoken yet to say that he would leave, and it was, therefore, even remotely possible that he would not. It was possible that he was just dressing so well to make himself feel better about waking to such a dark and hurtful night.

"Aunt Betty..."

Having merely heard the sound of her name in her nephew's voice, Anthony's kind, old aunt rose from her chair and went to him with a sobbing hug. "Oh, Anthony. I'm so sorry. He was much too young. Much too young."

Anthony did his best to comfort her, but he did so while holding her back a bit. It was clear to Eleanor that her husband did not want his shirt wrinkled or wept on, and so her mad hatred for *whomever it was* grew stronger.

"I know, Aunt Betty. I know." He pulled away from her now completely. "He's in a better place now." Anthony suddenly found himself glaring at his younger brother. "A far better place." He looked away, as if erasing his malicious stare, and he instantly looked back over to his brother. "James...," but he had no other words. He walked over to his brother's seat at the table, and James rose to embrace him. The two men hugged fiercely, but their affection did not linger. Eleanor could not help but notice that Anthony, immediately after breaking his hug with James, checked his beautiful, midnight-blue shirt to make sure that it was still tucked in properly and wrinkle-free. He then straightened his tie.

Why is he wearing a tie! Eleanor was now fuming. She felt a sudden pain from the force of her gnashed teeth, and she forced herself to relax them. *Please don't leave me, Anthony!*

65

"How are you doing with this, Anthony?" James asked darkly.

Anthony considered the question, and he looked away from James' caring eyes. "I'm all right. I guess." He looked back to his brother's stare. "I'll be feeling a bit better after a walk. I'm just gonna go get some air...clear my head a bit. I think I need to, before I let it all sink in."

I knew it! No! Please no! "I'll go with you," Eleanor offered in vain. "I could use some air myself." *I will kill you if say no. I will kill you if there's someone else.* She smiled at him innocently.

"No, El. Not tonight, if you don't mind. It's just...I really need to be alone right now. I've got to go walk my thoughts out...in solitude."

"Why? I'll be quiet. I just thought we could..."

"Oh, Eleanor dear. You're so sweet," Aunt Betty interrupted. "I know you want to shoulder this for him, but you've got to give him time to be by himself with what has happened."

You old bitch! How dare you talk to me like that! I'm not a child! And how dare you, Anthony, let her talk to me like that! I'm your wife! You should tell her to butt out!

"Aunt Betty's right, Eleanor. I won't be long. I just do better at sorting things out on lonely walks. That's all."

James spoke up, "Yes. Try to understand. Everyone must deal with grief in his or her own way."

Eleanor now hated both Betty and James for being so blind and stupid. She was amazed that neither of them had deduced that Anthony was leaving to meet up with someone else. He was lying to them, and they were both buying the whole load in the name of grief.

"Yes. And this is mine, El. You know that. I'm sorry to leave everyone so suddenly, but I'll be back in a little while. It's all going to be okay, you know." He offered a loving glance into his dear aunt's eyes, and he turned and walked out the back door.

Eleanor, not really caring how weak and desperate she would look to Betty and James, walked out after him and closed the door. "Anthony wait!"

Anthony turned to his wife with a look of nervous fear undisguised on his face. "Eleanor...I...what is it, love?"

Eleanor didn't want to make him angry. She didn't want to beg him to stay. She just wanted to make him *choose* to stay by showing him how much better she was than *whomever it was*. She was also lost to much reason in a state of sheer panic. "Anthony, I'm worried about you! It's so late, and I don't know this city. What if something happens to you? What will I do?"

Anthony smiled at his wife's concern. He laughed a little too. "Eleanor. Nothing is going to happen to me. I know this city very well. I grew up here, if you'll recall. I'll be back soon. I promise. Now go back inside, before Aunt Betty starts to think we're having marital problems."

Eleanor's disposition was unchanged by her husband's attempted levity. She glared at him sharply. "Aren't we?"

Anthony suddenly sobered. "No." He looked away. "I'll be back." Anthony then walked away from her.

"Anthony, where exactly are you going anyway? I need to know! Anthony!" *Please come back.*

He pretended not to hear her, as he walked out of the yard.

Seeing him walk out of sight, Eleanor held herself, as she slumped down on the porch and continued her mourning.

*   *   *   *

When Anthony arrived at David and Jonathan's, Tobit was waiting for him out front. The tall man smiled broadly at the sight of him. "Anthony! I knew you'd come."

Anthony returned the beautiful smile. "Hello, Tobit." Tobit then embraced Anthony and kissed him gently on the cheek. *This is so exhilarating,* Anthony thought, feeling his body tingle all over at the cold, forbidden touch of this elegant man. *I want him never to let me go.*

Tobit let Anthony go, and he smiled kindly. "You exhilarate me, too."

Anthony was startled. He felt somehow invaded, as if Tobit had been listening to his private thoughts. "What?"

"I said that I find you exhilarating, Anthony! I am very glad that you came back. I know it must have been difficult for you."

Anthony was reminded of the day's tragedy. "Yes. It was. I'm sorry it took so long. It's been a rough night."

"Yes, I know. I'm sorry about your friend."

Anthony was once again taken aback by Tobit's constant *knowing* of things. He asked in a slightly frightened voice, "How did you know about Derek?"

"He spoke of you, just before he died."

Anthony's eyes went wide with horror at the realization. Tobit had killed Derek! He was standing outside with a killer—a *vicious* killer!

Anthony locked onto Tobit's hypnotic eyes and seductive smile, and he was suddenly very calm. Tobit's eyes were now like a mother's hug to him. The thought of Derek dying at Tobit's hands now seemed only right. It was fitting and beautiful. Tobit was beautiful. He was an angel to Anthony. An angel of death perhaps, but an angel of beauty first and foremost. Anthony wanted Tobit with such a fierce passion that he could barely contain it. He wanted to worship Tobit, he wanted to belong to him and be loved by him. He wanted Tobit to touch and master every part of him—body, mind, and soul.

"Anthony, will you walk with me?"

Anthony smiled at Tobit and took his outstretched hand—the murder of Derek now lost to his immediate thoughts. "Yes."

Hand in hand the two walked away—forgetting the world behind them.

*   *   *   *

When the pair finally stopped, it was in front of James' church, and they sat on the steps outside of the unlocked sanctuary doors. Anthony sat across from Tobit and silently admired him in the moonlight, as the warm August breeze gently caressed his skin.

"Anthony, tell me about yourself."

Anthony was surprised at the request, but felt there was nothing he'd rather do than oblige. "Well, what do you want to know?"

"Just the important things. What have been your dreams? What have been your achievements?"

Anthony smiled, as he let his thoughts pass over his life. "I always wanted to be a great novelist, have a beautiful wife, many sons and daughters, a big house. I also wanted to be here tonight. I always dreamed of a man who would rescue me from myself before I dared to settle down with that beautiful wife of my fantasies. Another part of me wanted to be a priest, like my father. Like so many of my uncles down the line of my family tree. I wanted people to be proud of me. I wanted to be happy. But the two dreams could never be one. I could either be the ideal son and nephew, or I could be happy, like I am right now."

"You are at odds with yourself."

"Yes."

"Perhaps you think you can have it all?"

"No. I can't."

71

"What then, my beautiful friend? Where is your life taking you now?"

Anthony considered that. "I don't know. I don't even know where I am, as far as my life is concerned. I love Eleanor. I love her so much, and I want her to be happy, and I've vowed to be with her till death do us part. But, I can't say that I really want that at all. I can't say that I ever really did. At the same time, I don't want to leave her either. I don't want to fail her and everybody else. I've made the choice to be a husband, but even though I truly do love Eleanor, I have no love of having a wife. I mean, I suppose I love the idea of it. I love the idea that I'm doing what's right and what's expected. I love that everyone says, 'What a wonderful girl! Oh, your wife is so beautiful, however did you win her heart?' I love that people envy me, but I can't say in truth that I love *what* they envy.

"I love my family, but I stay away from them. I love the idea of being a priest, but I've grown to distrust the Church. I love and believe in God, but I don't know what He wants of me. I don't know why I have stray thoughts. I don't know why I'm here with you tonight. At the same time, if I was not here now, I'd be wondering just the same *why not?*

"I wanted to be a great novelist, and I told everyone when I went away to school that I was going to come back a rich man. Now, here I am eight years later, and I haven't written a single word outside of the newspaper in Nightfire. I have nothing original to say. There is nothing to write that has not already been written—nothing to say that has not already been said. So, I've sat there day after day at *The Nightfire Chronicle*, writing down what happened the day before, intimidated by the icons of my youth, like Anne Rice and Steven King, Isaac Asimov, and Richard Bach.

"Oh how I would dream of becoming the Jonathan Livingston Seagull of writers! With my pen I would write in just the same way that he flew, higher and higher, up into Heaven itself, and nothing would hold me back! Instead, I always stare at my blank page at home and think to myself, 'You're a fool to think you can compare to them, Anthony. Why even try? You'll just make a joke of yourself.' And I always put that novel off to the Eternal Tomorrow that never comes. Just as I always avoided speaking to the men who caught my eye. I didn't want to be rejected and mocked, but more importantly, I didn't want to betray my family, or my God. And I never became a priest, because I had to prove myself in so many other ways. I made it up to God by marrying Eleanor. That was to be my salvation, my penance for rejecting the long-standing family tradition of priesthood, and for having so many wicked thoughts."

Anthony sat, feeling the hardness of the stone steps beneath him and the gentle warmth of the sweet summer air, as he marveled at all he had said. He had never spoken those words aloud to anyone. He had never even allowed himself to think them so concretely. Anthony looked at Tobit, who sat smiling at him warmly, though Anthony knew those upturned lips to be quite cold. He thought of Derek, and was confused at himself for not saying anything before. The fear returned that Anthony had forgotten entirely during their walk. *His throat was ripped apart!* He spoke at last, timidly, "Are you going to kill me?"

Tobit laughed girlishly. "Never! I find you exquisite, and I would have you alive in this world forever!"

"Ah, if only you were God. I would never fear death."

Tobit spoke in a very strange tone—a tone that somehow enhanced his implacable accent, "Who is God?"

Anthony pondered the question, not knowing quite what Tobit had meant to imply, then he remembered Derek again. *Why is it so impossible to think of Derek without suddenly forgetting all about him?* "You killed Derek."

"No."

Anthony was confused, but said nothing.

Tobit finished his answer then, and Anthony was only further confused, "I took his life."

"How is that different?"

"It's all about how you look at it, Anthony. Had I taken a rock, smashed his skull, and left him to rot, then I would have simply killed him. I would have ended his life, nothing more nor less. But I did not simply end his life, I *took* it."

Anthony thought he understood, but he was not sure. His thoughts on the matter seemed to be slipping away. "Are you going to *take* my life?"

"No, but I would gladly *have* it. I want you very much, Anthony. Will you come into the church with me?"

Anthony found himself deeply aroused, and he had again forgotten all about Derek. The world was Tobit now, and nothing else could even hope to exist to him. Anthony stood and followed Tobit through the doors.

Once inside the church, Anthony made the sign of the cross and knelt down before the Virgin to pray. This particular church was rampant with decorations. The stained glass windows were brilliant and colorful, and there were foot-tall glass statues of various saints all around the sanctuary. When Anthony had finished praying, he lit a candle for Derek, he lit a candle for his Aunt Betty, Christopher, and Patches, he lit a candle for his brother James, and he lit a candle for Eleanor.

When he stood, Tobit was regarding him with amusement. "I thought you had no belief in the Church."

"I don't. But I do believe in prayer."

"Let's go into the sanctuary."

Without a word, Anthony nodded, glanced at the candles he had lit, and followed. Tobit went and stood at the front of the sanctuary where, on the altar, there rested a beautiful porcelain manger scene. Tobit studied it, and it seemed to Anthony that there was almost a look of contempt on his unscarred face. "Anthony, who is your God?"

"What do you mean?"

Tobit looked at him intently. "Who is it that you worship?"

Anthony fell deep into thought. He looked around the room. He studied the pictures of the windows in a quiet state of awe; he scoffed, just as silently, at the saints all around the sanctuary, but his eyes stopped and fixed on the eloquent, little manger scene that Tobit had found so worthy of study. He thought about the prayers he'd said as he'd entered the building. He thought about Who it was that he'd hoped would hear them, and he looked at the baby Jesus, lying in the hay. He looked at Mary—her hands placed over her heart as she smiled with a glow over the newborn King of Kings. He looked up at Tobit, who seemed almost sad now. "I worship Christ. He is my God."

Tobit shook his head sorrowfully, and he reached out, placing his hands on the back of Anthony's head, and he pulled Anthony closer, bringing the younger man's lips to his own. Anthony's passion burned ferociously as he felt the parting force of Tobit's delicious tongue between his lips. Anthony wrapped his arms around Tobit and gave in to the forbidden burn of his overpowering lust. He noticed the tastelessness of Tobit's mouth, and the exceptional sharpness of his teeth. He ran his fingers through Tobit's lustrous, beautiful hair as their yearning bodies were pressed ever more passionately together.

And without warning, Tobit broke the embrace completely. "I love you, Anthony. I want you. I want to be your only significant other. I want you to use the word love only for me. I want you to have me always first in your thoughts."

"Yes," Anthony said, trying to catch his breath. The sound of his own heartbeat now filled his ears. "Anything. Take me as you will, I love you already more than you can know!"

Tobit again shook his head sadly. "I am your god, Anthony."

"What?"

"*I* am your god. If we are to be together, that must be our first understanding. I am your god."

Anthony looked over at the manger scene on the altar, and then he looked over at Tobit. As he regarded Tobit, the heat of his passion again threatened to overwhelm him, and his manliness bulged behind the zipper of his pants with more eagerness and hunger than it had ever shown for Eleanor. Anthony wanted Tobit to finish the job. He was willing to do anything for this man. He wanted him more than God. He looked at Tobit's sad face, and the fire in his loins calmed, so that he could make a clear-headed choice. He looked again at the manger scene. He stepped up to it and picked up the delicate, glass Christ child. He turned it over in his hands, studied the baby's bright face, his arms reaching up to the Heavenly Father. Anthony looked Tobit in the eyes. "You are my god, Tobit. I will worship you with my every breath. Just let me love you. I want to love you." Anthony then pitched the infant figure with all of his might into the stone wall far behind Tobit, and he watched it shatter into countless porcelain shards.

Hearing the sound of the shattering idol, Tobit smiled and closed his eyes, as a tear escaped from one of them. He then stood poised, as if listening devotedly to something, though Anthony heard nothing. "Can you hear it? Isn't that the most beautiful music?"

Anthony was perplexed. "What music? There isn't any music here."

Tobit opened his eyes and smiled affectionately at his lovely companion. "Yes, Anthony, there is always music in a church. The Chorus of Angels rings throughout any place of faith, and around any person of faith. This church is a place of continual faith and holiness. Corrupt as its priests and popes may have been through the centuries, the people still hold it sacred. Listen."

"I don't hear anything."

Tobit walked over to Anthony, until Anthony could feel the taller man's breath on his face. "I will help you." Tobit again took Anthony in a powerful kiss, and as Anthony recognized the very slight taste of his own blood in Tobit's mouth, he could suddenly hear the most beautiful arrangement of "Ave Maria" flowing through his ears. There were voices singing, but no words, only melody, harmony, the very sound of beauty itself. As Anthony listened to the glorious song, and let his body writhe to the rhythm of Tobit's passion, his arm flew back and knocked the porcelain Virgin from the altar, causing it to shatter on the floor by their feet.

Tobit stood back and giggled like a child. "Who is your god, Anthony?"

"You are, Tobit. Only you."

Tobit reached out and loosened Anthony's tie. He then used it to pull Anthony forward, and he kissed him quickly on the lips. "Will you meet me again tomorrow? There is more still, if we are to be together."

"Yes, of course. I live for you. But what about tonight?"

"Tonight," Tobit said seductively, "we shall desecrate the house of your brother's god." Tobit ripped open Anthony's shirt and felt the tightly sculpted muscles of his torso.

Anthony quivered with desire at Tobit's frigid touch. He reached out for him, and Tobit kissed him with more passion than any times previous.

As Anthony and his forbidden lover defiled the church of his former god with their pleasure, the candles in the entryway were quietly blown out by a mysterious, indoor breeze.

3

Eleanor entered the guest room to find Anthony still writing in his journal. He had barely spoken to her the whole day, and now it was almost over. She had gone upstairs and sobbed herself to sleep shortly after he had left the night before, and when she woke up this morning, he had already gone out to buy a nice suit for Derek's funeral. When he had finally returned, at around five, he had taken a quick, silent lunch with Betty and Christopher, and then he had gone upstairs to write. Eleanor decided that she was going to make him talk to her, now that he had been upstairs for nearly three hours. "Still writing?"

Anthony made a few more quick scratches with his pen before putting it down with a great sigh of satisfaction. "Just finished." He looked at her with affectionate eyes. "What's up?"

"Nothing. So what time did you get home last night?"

"I don't know. Pretty late I guess."

"Where did you go?"

Anthony shrugged and laughed it off. "Oh, all around. You know."

"I see." She avoided his lying gaze. "So have you decided to be sad about Derek yet?"

"What? Of course I'm sad. What the hell do you mean? You're not still upset because I went walking without you?"

"No. I just meant that you've seemed unusually preoccupied, and I can't help but notice that there isn't much around here for you to be preoccupied with, except for your late-night adventures. James told me that you went walking for a long time on Monday as well."

"What exactly are you trying to imply, Eleanor? I haven't done anything terrible. It's just nostalgia. I like to walk around the neighborhood and remember what it was like to be a boy here."

"Maybe you'd like to take Patches with you. You used to tell me how he was always at your side."

"Patches would rather stay with Christopher, I'm sure. Besides, he's old now. I wouldn't want to wear him out."

Eleanor realized that she was not going to get any answers out of him, and she decided to turn the conversation. "It's good to see you writing again. It's been a long time since you opened your journal."

Anthony closed the notebook and looked over at her. "Yes. I suppose it has. I guess it's been a while since anything noteworthy has happened."

"Oh, I see. That must have been some spectacular clothing store you went to today."

Anthony did not fail to see the sarcasm. "Eleanor, please get a grip. I can't handle this right now. Why are you always so suspicious? I was writing down my thoughts about being back in Houston after so many years—the way that so much has changed, and yet remained the same. It's not like I'm having an affair!"

"Who said anything about an affair? Those were your words, not mine."

"God damn it, El!" Anthony took a deep breath and collected himself. "Let's go downstairs. I'm starving. Besides, I don't want to seem anti-social."

Could have fooled me. "All right." Anthony took Eleanor's arm lovingly in his own and led her out the door. As she walked out, she dared a glance back and, to her satisfaction, the journal was still out on the room's little desk. If Anthony felt the need to take another walk tonight, and she knew that he would, she hoped that he did not think to hide that journal first.

*   *   *   *

The couple entered the kitchen in silence and sat down at the table with Christopher. Aunt Betty was at the sink washing dishes. Christopher looked up at Anthony, who was seated directly across from him, and he clumsily shuffled a worn-looking deck of cards. "Wanna play poker, Cousin Anthony?"

Anthony at once forgot his bad mood and looked in wonder over at the small child. "Poker? Um, no. I never play poker with anyone that doesn't have a job."

"Can't playing poker be my job?"

Anthony and Eleanor both started laughing hysterically. Aunt Betty stopped doing her dishes and looked over at the lad scornfully. "Aunt Betty,"

Anthony asked, "are you *sure* this isn't Ben's son? I mean, he and Trixie could have been kissin' cousins."

"Your cousin Benjamin is a fine lawyer and above such criminal notions as career poker playing!"

"Sure, *now*. But when he was younger..."

"Christopher, I think it's past your bed time."

"Aw! Aunt Betty! Can't I stay up and play poker with Cousin Anthony? He has a job!"

Aunt Betty was horrified. "Christopher! Where did you ever learn to play poker?"

Anthony answered for the boy, "James."

Aunt Betty glared at Anthony, though she could not hide the crooked smile on her face. "Anthony, did you teach him to play poker?"

Anthony held his hands up in the air. "Not me! I wouldn't go near this kid with a deck of cards. He'd probably take me for all I'm worth!"

"Damn straight, Cousin."

"Christopher! We do not use dirty words in this house! And we *especially* do not use dirty words in front of ladies! You apologize to your cousins right now!"

Christopher looked very hurt by Aunt Betty's scolding. He stuck his lower lip out as far as it would go. "I'm sorry, Cousin Anthony." He

86

looked over to Eleanor and smiled broadly. "I'm sorry, Cousin Eleanor."

"No offense, Kid," Anthony offered sympathetically.

"It's all right, Christopher. It was just an accident," Eleanor said.

Christopher looked at Eleanor with a very serious expression now on his face. "Aunt Betty says that you and Anthony will be married until one of you dies. Is that true?"

Eleanor smiled nervously, actually wondering if she and Anthony were going to make it that long. "Yes. Of course it's true."

"Oh. Well, when Anthony dies, can *I* marry you?"

Anthony laughed harder than he had laughed in days, and Eleanor blushed miserably.

Aunt Betty again scolded Christopher, as she dished up a plate of food for Anthony, "Christopher Allen Paul! That was a very rude thing to say!"

"Why? Anthony thought it was funny!" Christopher joined Anthony in laughter, though he did not really understand the humor himself.

"I'll talk to you about it later. It's past your bed time now, so say goodnight to your cousins, and wake Patches up off the floor."

Christopher kicked the old dog in the back. "Come on, Patches! Get up. It's bed time, and you gotta come keep me warm!"

Patches sat up with a start and looked around. He then saw that it was Christopher who had kicked him, and he relaxed and wagged his tired, old tail.

"Come 'ere, Patches," Anthony commanded. The dog got up and obeyed, and Anthony scratched him behind his matted ears with deep affection. "Good boy. Good. You taking good care of Christopher? I know you are. You always took good care of me."

Christopher seemed to take great interest in Anthony and Patches, but he remained quiet.

Aunt Betty put a plate full of food in front of Anthony. "Aunt Betty, you know I don't eat cabbage!"

"Anthony, you need more vegetables in your diet! You can't live on meat and potatoes alone! I will not have you malnourished while you're staying in my home."

Anthony looked over to Christopher and made a sickly face. Christopher giggled at this.

"And you must show Christopher that even big boys eat their cabbage. He doesn't like it either."

"Oh, all right. I'll eat it. See, Christopher, you only have to put up with this 'till you can drive. Then you go get a burger and fries every night you can. No cabbage. But see, what happens if you don't let Aunt Betty feed you cabbage is she feeds you squid instead."

"Nu-uh!"

"Uh-huh! I swear! Live squid! If you think cabbage is bad, you've got another thing coming, buddy." Anthony put the first bite of cabbage in his mouth and made an absolutely horrible face as he chewed. Christopher giggled like the child he was. When Betty turned around to get back to her dishes, Anthony secretively showed Christopher the trick of the trade. He whispered, "Here you go, Patches," and he hand fed a palm-full of cabbage to the dog, who quickly spit it out and tried to forget it had ever been in his mouth. "He doesn't like it either." Christopher began to giggle ferociously at this.

Aunt Betty turned off the water and turned around sharply. "Anthony Alexander Paul! Are you feeding your cabbage to Patches!"

The dog looked to Aunt Betty with his ears cocked, and Anthony did his best to look innocent, but Christopher's giggle gave him away. Eleanor slapped her husband playfully.

"All right, Christopher. Go on to bed. I'll be in to tuck you in and say your prayers in a few minutes."

Christopher slid out of his chair and started to walk out, but then paused. "Can Anthony tuck me in tonight?"

Aunt Betty seemed surprised. "Well, I suppose you should ask him."

Christopher looked over to his cousin.

"Sure, Kid. I'll be right there." Anthony fed Patches a sliver of meat from his plate and mussed the creature's hair as he ate. "Go on, Patches."

"Come on, Patches! Let's go to bed!" Patches walked over happily to Christopher. "Cousin Anthony?"

"Yeah."

"When you come tuck us in, will you tell me a story about you and Patches? When you were kids?"

Eleanor covered her beaming grin of adoration at the whole scenario, and Anthony Answered with a very charmed smile, "Sure, Kid. That'll be great. See you in a few minutes."

"Okay. Good night, Aunt Betty."

"Good night, Christopher. Sweet dreams," she answered him.

"Good night, pretty Eleanor."

Eleanor giggled with disbelief at the small child's persistence. "Good night, Christopher. Don't let the bed bugs bite."

Christopher was horrified. "Bugs?"

Aunt Betty was quick to the rescue. "It's just a figure of speech, dear. Go on to bed now, and we'll see you in the morning."

"Oh." Christopher turned with Patches and walked out of the kitchen and up the stairs to his room. "Good night, everybody!"

"Oh, he's just so sweet," Aunt Betty commented once the boy had left. "No telling how many bad habits he picked up during his brief time with Trixie. I'll straighten that boy out if it kills me. I am determined."

"I know you will, Aunt Betty. You're the best. You worked wonders for me."

"Really? Then eat your cabbage. You need vegetables. Eleanor, make sure he eats his vegetables every night when you get to Colorado. He won't do it if he isn't forced, and his colon will fall right out one of these days."

Eleanor leaned over and held the love of her life, putting her head on his shoulder. "I'll take care of him. You're so good with children, Anthony."

"Hey, I owe it all to her. She was good with me and James, and Ben and Trixie when they would visit."

Aunt Betty was obviously a little bit embarrassed by the compliment. "Eat your dinner, Anthony. I don't want it to get cold now."

"All right, Aunt Betty. Whatever you say, dear." Anthony ate his food without another word.

The back door suddenly opened, and James walked in. "Hello, everyone! Is there food?"

"Of course there's food, dear. I always cook enough for an army or two. It's a habit I developed during your teen years."

"Oh, it smells good, Aunt Betty."

Anthony spoke from the table, "That's because it is good, dumb-ass."

James was indignant. "Anthony, is it really necessary to use that kind of language?"

"Oh, come on, James. What is it with you? Is that collar chokin' out your sense of humor?"

"You sound like Derek."

"I'm making up for his absence."

James surprised Anthony by smiling. "I'm glad. I don't know what it's going to be like without him around."

Aunt Betty came at James with a plate of food, heavy on the cabbage. He made a face, as if he'd just inhaled something odious. "Cabbage?"

"Don't even start with me! How are things at the church?"

James set his plate down at Christopher's now vacant spot at the table, and he sat. "Well, sort of odd actually. There was some vandalism last night in the sanctuary. When we asked old Father Maxwell about it, he said that he heard the noise and went to the peep hole to see what was going on. When we pressed him for what he saw, he got all fidgety, and said and swore that he saw a man at the altar, standing with the devil. He said he saw them kissing, and they smashed the Virgin Mary from the manger scene. Upon seeing this, he didn't call the police, he went to his bed and prayed.

"I'll tell you, it was difficult to be understanding. Actually, I don't know what to think. At first I tried to convince him that he had been dreaming, but the evidence was more in his favor. I'm afraid he's just going a bit senile. It's very sad. He's been at our church for five years, and all generations there love him like a grandfather. If nothing else, I won't question that he truly *believes* that he saw the devil—Satan himself, in our sanctuary last night. Crazy. He even went so far as to say that he'd met the devil before, when he was eighteen years old, and that he had rejected him and all of his pleasures, but never forgot his face."

James paused to see everyone staring at him with their full attention. It was something he was not used to. He noticed that none seemed so bothered by his tale as his older brother Anthony. "I don't know," he continued. "What am I supposed to think? I mean, I can't deny the existence of Satan, but...how often does he stop by and vandalize the church, in person, in the middle of the night? It's just difficult to accept, and I don't know whether or not it's something that I *should* accept. Father Maxwell is very old after all."

As old as temptation. Anthony stood up quickly, his face very pale. "I've got to go take care of Christopher and Patches. I'll be back."

Eleanor looked forlorn as soon as Anthony had left the room. James spoke again, "Maybe it's just because I haven't seen him in four years, but does anyone else think that Anthony is acting a bit strange?"

Eleanor looked suddenly relieved. "Yes. Thank God it's not just me!"

Betty found herself defensive over Anthony. "Well of course he's behaving strangely. He's just lost his best friend to a horrible death! His throat was ripped out! I'm surprised we're not all at the edge. Can you imagine a person that would do such a violent thing to another man? Simply horrifying! And to think they don't even know who did it. Yes.

Anthony has every right to be a little bit shaken, under the circumstances."

"Hm," James thought out loud. "Maybe the devil *has* come to town." He looked at his aunt. "Can I have some milk?"

*   *   *   *

Twenty minutes later, Anthony returned from putting Christopher to sleep. He looked more haunted than ever, and all eyes could see. "Please excuse me. I need to take another walk." He looked at his wife, expecting an argument, or an accusation, but none came.

"I know. This is hard on you, isn't it? The funeral tomorrow morning?" Eleanor smiled innocently up at him.

"Yes. I'm sorry."

"Don't apologize, dear. I want you to do whatever it takes to get through this funeral tomorrow. I'm glad you *can* walk out your emotions every night. I'm happy that you're handling this as well as you are."

She continued to smile, and Anthony found himself not trusting it somehow. "Thank you," he said. "I won't be long."

James spoke up, "Of course, that's what you said last night too, and you weren't even back before I left." He smiled lovingly at his nervous brother.

Aunt Betty was instantly on her feet. "Anthony, you look terrible!" She put a hand on his forehead, and he backed away.

"I'm all right, Aunt Betty. Stop motherin' me; I'm twenty-six."

"It doesn't matter, Anthony. Twenty-six-year-olds still have allergies. How are yours? Are you feeling sick? Do you need some anti-biotic?"

Anthony laughed. "No, Aunt Betty. I'm fine. I'll be great once I get some air."

"Anthony, don't fib to me now. You've had summer allergies all your life. Are you sure they aren't upsetting you?"

"Aunt Betty, would I be going for a walk if they were? Thank you for your great concern. I love you," he leaned over and kissed her worry-creased forehead, "but I got a shot in May. I'm fine. I'll see y'all later." Anthony walked out the door.

Eleanor wasted no time in excusing herself. "If nobody minds, I think I'm going to turn in early tonight. I want to be wide awake tomorrow morning. I hate funerals."

"Of course, Eleanor," Aunt Betty said. "I don't blame you at all."

"Thank you. Good night, family. I'll see you in the morning." Eleanor then left the kitchen and climbed the stairs to her room.

"Oh, what a wonderful, kind, and understanding wife she is," Aunt Betty said with a hand over her heart.

"Yes," James agreed. "Anthony is very lucky."

*   *   *   *

That lying, stupid bastard! Eleanor thought as she opened the journal still resting on the little guest room desk. *Now we'll see what's really so great about his damned walks!* She flipped through to the last written-on page and then flipped back to the beginning of the entry. She read the pages in horror.

August 16, 1995

Again I write to better know my inner thoughts. I have reached a point in my life in which I do not know whether I'm lost or found. I know only that I have changed, and whether for better or worse, I know this change in me to be irrevocable. I have fallen passionately in love, and for the object of my love there is nothing that I am not willing to do. Unfortunately, this love has come to me after having been married to someone else for two months now.

I am so confused. I suppose it would do me good to recount the story in full:

I arrived in Houston with my lovely wife just two days ago. We stopped for an indeterminately long visit with my Aunt Betty before our move to Colorado, where I am to settle for the life of an English teacher, having failed to ever produce one word of decent fiction, and having seen my hours kept at the newspaper in Nightfire as unfit for starting a family of my own.

On the first night spent here, in the house of my lost youth, I got into a bitter argument with my brother James. Maybe there was a part of me that wanted to do so—for old times' sake. I doubt I'll ever know. In anger, I stormed out of the house, and I went wandering down the path I would follow in the rage of my teens. To the bad part of the neighborhood, as Aunt Betty always saw it.

I braved, for the first time, the forbidden bar of fantasies past. It was then that I met Tobit—an angel to my innocent eyes, but a monster none the less. Our mutual attraction was instant, and he made me promise to meet him again on the following night, which I did.

So last night, as agreed, I met him again, and I found the most liberating night of my entire adult life!

It was on this night that I learned of my life-long friend Derek Andrews' demise. And I learned that the murderer had in fact been the Tobit that I'd come to love! This brings us to a point that troubles me to no end, and confuses me. Whenever I am with Tobit, it is as though all thoughts of loss for Derek were being blocked. I can not seem to focus for more than a few seconds, or to ponder the actuality of Tobit's murderous ways. I am so deeply troubled by this, because when I am here, or anywhere for that matter that Tobit is not, I am deeply grievous over the loss of my friend. I can not stand the thought of a world without him! I want to ask Tobit, "Why did you kill him! What do you want of <u>me</u>!" But I don't. When I'm with Tobit, there is nothing but Tobit to me, and I love that about him. He is my tempter and my corrupter. I belong to Tobit! I want him to master me in every way!

Especially after last night.

Last night, we went to the church of my boyhood, and I abandoned Christ for him—in both word and action. I gave my soul to Tobit. And then, we consummated our passion. How can I say it? We made love...without making love. No words can describe it! It was unequivocal ecstasy!

I told him my dreams and failures, and he was understanding. He still wants me, as I want him, and he shall have me, in whatever way he requests of me. I will do anything he asks. Anything! He is my god now! He is my Christ.

Eleanor closed the book in tears of both sorrow and rage. She was so destroyed, and she wished that she had never read the journal at all. No matter how suspicious she had been before, she had never expected anything quite so terrible as what she had discovered in her husband's confessions. She wanted death. She wanted death for everyone. She was crushed—her bones, she felt, ground into powder. There was no hope, no salvation, no turning back. It was over. Her marriage, her life—everything. Her husband had found love in the arms of another—another man at that! A man with whom not even God could compete in the eyes of Anthony. There was nothing that could be done.

Eleanor folded herself up on the bed and cried, in physical pain, until her aching head ceased to know consciousness and carried her away to dreams not half as horrible as the reality that they had helped her to escape; but horrible just the same. There was no real escape for her now. Her smile had died, and would never bloom again.

*   *   *   *

Anthony walked through the doors of David and Jonathan's, again greeted by the up-beat sounds of current pop artists flying from the speakers placed all around the room. The place was much busier than it had been the first time he'd entered it, and Anthony noticed the very interested eyes of several patrons glued to his beautiful form. All this meant nothing to him. He was looking only for Tobit, who came up behind him like a ghost in the crowd. "Hello, Anthony!"

Anthony turned around. "Tobit! I was beginning to fear you'd made other plans."

"Never. Shall we go?"

"Sure."

The two left the crowded bar and took to the quiet streets. The air was warm as it should be, and Anthony felt all the warmer for being in the presence of Tobit. They walked to an undeveloped lot of land—a veritable forest—in which pine trees seemed to reach the stars. They walked deep into the little forest, until they came to an open space, where the moonlight glowed with considerable glory. "Tobit?"

The taller man responded as he rested himself on a fallen tree, "Yes, love?"

"Are you the devil?"

Tobit did not laugh, as Anthony had hoped that he would. Rather, he seemed to take the question very seriously. "I do not think so."

"Are you saying that you don't know?"

"No. I am saying that I do not believe myself to be the devil. I am not Satan. However, I could see myself being mistaken for the devil. I could be the devil to some, if they chose to see me as such. If you give it honest consideration, *you* could even be mistaken for the devil—if only for being in the woods late at night, wanting very much to make love to your beautiful, male companion." Tobit smiled, and the moonlight on his pale skin gave him the illusion of glowing in the darkness as he did so. "Why do you ask? Do you think that I'm Satan himself? Am I that horrific to you?" Tobit suddenly looked sad.

"No," Anthony insisted. "I know you're not Satan, but in truth I don't know who you *are!* You've told me nothing of yourself. I don't know

where you came from, I can't place that accent, I
don't know what you do for a living, I don't
know...how old you are." *As old as temptation...*
"Maybe you *are* the devil."

Tobit stood and went to his young friend.
"Anthony." He reached out and caressed Anthony's smooth, unscarred face. "Do you love me?"

"Yes," Anthony said, as if the question had hurt
him.

"And do you know that I love you?"

"Yes, I do."

Tobit smiled. "Then, if you were to discover
that I were the very devil himself, honestly, would
it really matter to you at all?"

Anthony looked away, as he considered that,
and turned back to Tobit's loving eyes with his
answer, "No."

Tobit's smile broadened, and he leaned over to
kiss Anthony on the mouth. "Then why are we
having this conversation at all?" He giggled at Anthony's troubled expression. Then his own expression went dark. "Anthony, now I have a question
that I must ask you. There are so many things
that must be made clear between us, if we are
to be together for all time."

"Anything, Tobit. What is it you wish to know?"

Tobit looked away, sadly. "Who is it that nurtures
you, Anthony?"

"What do you mean?"

"When you think of someone caring for you, who is it that comes to mind? Who do you see as your care-taker, your guardian, your role-model?"

Anthony considered that for a long moment. He pondered the words. *Nurture, caring, guardian, role-model...Aunt Betty.* Of course it was his Aunt Betty. He thought of all the times he'd scraped his knees and broken bones as a child. He remembered what a relatively frail child he had been for all the trouble he'd gotten into. He thought of all the bee stings she'd treated, the cabbage she'd forced him to eat, the way she wouldn't let him leave, even on this very night, until she was sure his allergies were taken care of. He smiled. "My Aunt Betty. She has always nurtured me." He met Tobit's somber gaze. "She has always been the very picture of caring, to my eyes."

Tobit shook his head sadly, and Anthony's smile faded as the tall man spoke, "No, Anthony. *I* nurture you. When you think of these things: nurturing, care-taking, and the like, you must think only of me. There can be only me as your guardian, if we are to be together. Do You understand?"

Anthony did. "Yes. I understand."

"Then you know what you have to do?"

"Yes. Anything for you, Tobit."

Tobit smiled, and again a teardrop fell from both his eyes. "I love you, Anthony. Tonight, I will give you pleasure, and we will part early so that you can take care of things at home before the funeral tomorrow. Then, tomorrow night, I will show you one of my tricks. I will not meet you at the bar, but I will find you wherever you go."

"Yes. Let me love you now. I must show you my love, Tobit! I am yours."

"You make me very happy, Anthony. I am very proud of you. Let me nurture you now."

"Yes."

Tobit snatched Anthony up in a powerful embrace, and Anthony was led to explore, through Tobit, his deepest capacity for love and pleasure.

*   *   *   *

Anthony returned home at 2:07 AM to find all lights out, and all at home in bed. He looked around at the small kitchen, and he thought about all the meals his dear aunt had prepared for him since the time of his boyhood. He remembered how she had always welcomed his friends to the table with open arms and never a complaint. He looked at the sink, and his memories took him to all the times he'd stood over that sink as Aunt Betty poured peroxide on his many scrapes and childhood wounds. He looked around, he remembered, and he said good-bye.

Anthony walked around the stairwell and slowly opened Aunt Betty's bedroom door. It creaked ever so slightly, but the sound failed to wake his well worn out Aunt Betty. Anthony stood at the foot of her bed, as she slept so peacefully. He wondered briefly what that must be like—to sleep so peacefully. Anthony stood and watched her as she breathed. He studied the arms that had so often hugged him in times of his greatest desperation, the lips that had countless times kissed him on the cheek as he'd gone out the door for school. He remembered these things, and he said good-bye.

Anthony walked quietly over to the other side of Betty's large bed, and then he returned to her side with an adequate pillow in hand. He made not a sound as he slowly, yet forcefully, put the pillow over his sleeping aunt's face.

Anthony watched as his loving aunt suffocated under his determined strength. He watched her die in a state of fear, panic, and absolute helplessness. Throughout the house, not a sound was heard.

*   *   *   *

As Anthony entered the guest room, he looked at his beautiful wife as she slept. He found himself proud, as always, to have captured such a beauty. He knew that he had been the envy of James and Derek the second he'd walked into the kitchen holding her hand. Anthony stared at her for quite some time, before he removed his grass-stained clothes. He then crawled into bed beside her and covered both her and himself, as she had not bothered to cover herself before, with a warm blanket—a quilt, actually, that his Aunt Betty had made with his mother, his grandmother, his great-grandmother, and his Aunt Amanda many years before his own birth. He wrapped a strong arm around his sleeping wife, and he fell asleep, wondering if children would be in their future, or if Tobit could fill that void as well.

4

"When will Aunt Betty be back?" Christopher asked for the hundredth time.

"I don't know, honey. Nobody told me that." Anthony had forced Eleanor to get out of bed— something she had never wanted to do again— just in time to get ready for Derek's funeral. He had explained to her that Betty had gone to meet Trixie somewhere to discuss Christopher's future, and she would not be back for several days. Not knowing the town, and receiving no aid from

Anthony, Eleanor had been given no alternatives to taking the child to the funeral with them. Finding funerals impossible enough to get through on their own, Eleanor was not in the least bit pleased to have to care for a six-year-old in addition. She thought his stream of ignorant questions would never end. *How long will Derek be dead? When are you going to die, Cousin Eleanor? Will you die before I do? What are they going to do with him until he stops being dead? How far away is Heaven? Did Darth Vader go to Heaven too?*

"Will she be back before I'm dead?"

Eleanor laughed in spite of her dark mood. "Yes, Christopher. I'm sure of that much." She smiled at him, as she sat on the living room couch and scratched Patches on the head. Her feelings towards the old beast had definitely changed over the past few days. She now felt a sort of kinship with the creature. *Anthony has left us both.*

"When will Cousin Anthony be back?"

Eleanor tensed. "I don't know, Christopher. He likes his walks very much these days."

"Do you think he might be dead?"

Eleanor's eyes glazed over. "Not yet." She suddenly needed to be alone. She stood. "I'll be right back. You and Patches play."

Eleanor walked into the kitchen, and she braced herself on the counter. She couldn't allow herself to cry. Not in front of the child. She just knew that if she did, he would never stop asking her questions about it. *Oh, Anthony, why are you doing this to me? Oh I wish I were a man! Why does it have to be a man? What did I do wrong? I can try...I can be man enough...*

Eleanor shook her head to clear it. She stood back, opened a drawer, and removed from it a very long and sharp knife. She turned it over in her hand, and she considered the infinite uses to which it could be put.

*   *   *   *

Anthony stood at the freshly laid grave of Derek Andrews, and he thought about all the day's pain. *Why, Tobit? Why did you kill him?* Anthony pondered the mysteries of life and death, and he recalled his brother's words on the night he had arrived in town. The words he had spoken to Derek: *If you were to die tonight, I'd fear for your soul as well.* Anthony wondered if James had remembered saying those words to Derek at the funeral; for, as it turned out, Derek had died that night— not half an hour after James had pronounced him damned.

Anthony stared up at the few stars permitted by the city lights of Houston, and he wondered after Derek's soul.

"Hello, Anthony."

Anthony gasped, turned around, and clutched his rapidly beating heart. "Shit! You scared the life out of me."

"I'm sorry. I thought you'd be expecting me. I told you I would find you."

Anthony noticed that, for once, the appearance of Tobit had not fogged over his thoughts of Derek. He looked menacingly into Tobit's eyes. "Why did you kill Derek? How did you find me here? And why is it that whenever you're around I can't hate you for killing him!"

Tobit looked deeply wounded, and, turning, he began silently to weep.

Anthony felt a sudden surge of guilt at having stricken his sweet Tobit with such accusing words. "I'm sorry, Tobit. Please forgive me."

He kissed his lover lightly on the cheek. "I've had a difficult day."

"Yes. I know. I told you...I was sorry to have taken your friend's life. I didn't care for him as you did. He was nothing more than a blade of grass to me—and I the grazing lamb. I had no malicious intent."

111

"I understand." Anthony wasn't actually sure that he did, but he was trying earnestly, for love of Tobit.

"I do not wish for you to think of him when we are together, because I fear that you will hate me. I fear that you will see me as a monster, when I am not. I am no more a monster than you are, Anthony. I have feelings just as you do."

Anthony was hanging his head in shame. "Please, Tobit. Forgive me. You know that I love you more than anything. You are my god and my savior. You are the healer of my pain—my guardian and care-taker."

Tobit's spirits seemed lifted by this. He turned to Anthony with a weak smile. "You still want for us to be together then?"

"Yes," Anthony pleaded, "more than anything!"

"And you know that there is still more for you to do before we can be one?"

"Yes. I'll do anything you will for me to do, my love. My one true love."

Tobit's pain was gone now, and he spoke with sparks of cleverness and glee, "I know that there is one question on your mind, and you will not rest until you ask it. So ask it, I beg you, and then we shall begin."

Anthony looked both startled and relieved. He thought that if he asked this question, Tobit's answer, whatever that answer may be, would resolve the torment of his heart. He asked, "Has Derek gone to Heaven?"

A somberness shaded Tobit's face, as he looked his lover in the eyes and spoke with haunting certainty, "No." He shook his head with quiet compassion. "There is no Heaven. Human souls have made Hell so vast that there is no *room* for Heaven."

Anthony's heart sank, and yet he felt relief as well. It was resolved. He knew the fate of Derek's soul, for Tobit had spoken. And James had been right. And now, Anthony knew that every soul on Earth was unconditionally damned.

"Are you happy, Anthony? Are you happy to be with me?"

Anthony looked up, taken from his thoughts and again feeling hurt by any question of his love for Tobit. "Yes, Tobit. You *are* my happiness! And I know that there is a question on your mind as well. And you will not rest until you've heard my answer. Because I do now know you well." Anthony smiled with nothing but love in his manner. "And I pray you also know me well. For there is nothing that I would not do for you, my love."

Tobit's smile shined brighter than the stars. "You do know me well, Anthony. And you know that I want nothing more than for us to be together always."

"Yes. Nor is there anything on Earth that I myself want more."

Tobit continued to smile, as he put his arms around his lover's neck and drew himself closer to him. "Then, if we are to be together, there is something else that must be clear between us."

"Anything, Tobit."

"I must know. I know that it is I you worship, and that it is I who nurtures you. Now I must know, who is it that *you* nurture? Who is it that you feel looks up to you and sets you as a role model? Who trusts you above all others and looks to you when they are in need of teaching, repair, or comforting?"

Anthony considered the question as he had the night before, and his mind took him easily to his faithful Patches. He remembered how he'd risked life and limb to rescue the hungry, little pup so many years ago. He thought of Patches, throughout his youth, following at his heals, waiting for instructions. Patches, frightened by a storm, crawling under the covers with him. Patches waiting on young Anthony to feed him, to walk him, to love him unconditionally. Then Anthony thought of Christopher, who now took care of Patches. He thought of how Christopher now looked to him to know *how* to care for Patches, to see what big boys did and how they were to act. *Can Anthony tuck me in tonight?* It was easy to see that, over the past few days, Anthony had become the boy's greatest role model. It was also undeniable that Patches had learned his every trick and trait from Anthony over the course of their years together. When Anthony thought of nurturing and guiding people, he thought most strongly of Patches...and now also of Christopher. The boy and his dog.

Anthony stared into Tobit's loving eyes. "Patches and Christopher look to me for all of life's answers. I nurture Christopher now, and have always nurtured Patches in the past."

Tobit's eyes grew sad, and he spoke to Anthony tenderly, "When I arrived tonight, you stopped my hurt tears with your love. I showed you my trick of finding you tonight so that you might be pleased with me and impressed. I sought your approval, and I need to hear you speak of my beauty in order to believe in it myself. It is *I* that you nurture, Anthony. And, if we are to be together, it can be *only* I that you nurture. Do you see?"

"Yes," Anthony said. "Only you, my beautiful Tobit. And I know what must be done. I love you, and I will sacrifice everything to you. I now nurture *only* you." Anthony smiled, and a tear left his eye as though he'd had the most glorious of spiritual revelations, and a great burden had at long last been lifted from his back.

Tobit's joy was overwhelming, and he embraced Anthony with still more passion than the younger man had ever known.

*   *   *   *

Anthony entered the old house to find everyone still awake. He thought of what it would take to get his wife to leave the room. He walked over to where she sat on the couch, glaring at him, and he surprised her with a kiss on the lips and a gentle smile.

"Anthony, are you all right?"

"Never better, El. I love you." He then leaned over to her ear and whispered, "Would you wait for me in bed? It's been too long since we've behaved like Bride and Groom."

She nodded her head, not quite knowing what to think. Had she read a work of fiction in his journal? Perhaps he had only fantasized about meeting Derek's killer. Perhaps the journal entry he'd written had only been a way to cope with his grief. Perhaps his eyes had never strayed at all.

He smiled with approval at her. "I'll put the kids to bed." He kissed her again. "Go on."

Eleanor rose with confusion. "Good night, men. I'll see you in the morning."

Christopher was confused by the suddenness with which his pretty "cousin" had rushed off to bed. She'd seemed wide awake enough before Anthony had returned. He looked to Anthony. "Do I have to go to bed now too?"

Anthony smiled at the child. "No. Not just yet. I have something for you and Patches."

The child lit up like a star. "What?"

"Midnight snacks! Wait here, and I'll call you in a minute."

"A real minute, or a grown-up minute?" Christopher asked with suspicion.

Anthony grinned. "A real minute, I promise. Just wait here."

Anthony then went off to the kitchen, where he opened the highest cabinet in the room. He remembered that Aunt Betty, living so near the "edge of the civilized world," would frequently have problems with rats, but she was always very quick to stop such problems the moment they began. He rummaged around on tip-toe, until he found what he was looking for. A sigh of satisfaction left him as he removed the rat Poison from the cabinet and set it on the counter. He then opened a can of dog food and made the preparations for Patches' final meal. "Patches! Come 'ere, boy! Here, Patches!"

In the living room, the old dog's ears cocked at the energetic call of his master's voice. He looked at Christopher, then back to the kitchen, and he jumped to his feet and trotted off.

"Can I come too, Anthony?"

"Not yet, Chris. Hold on just a little longer!"

As Patches entered the kitchen to see his beloved master holding his bowl full of food by the uncharacteristically open garage door, he slowed his pace, and then stopped.

"Come on, Patches! Don't you want your midnight snack?"

Patches suddenly wore the most human look of distrust on his face. He looked back to the living room, as if concerned for Christopher, then he looked back to Anthony and growled lowly.

Anthony found himself frightened by this. Patches had never growled at him before, and it was likely to upset his simple plan of pleasing Tobit. "Patches. What's the matter? Don't you trust me?"

At the pleading sound of Anthony's voice, the dog growled just a decibel louder. Fearful that Christopher would hear and become suspicious,

Anthony put the bowl down on the table and said, "Okay, look. It's okay. You don't have to eat it."

Patches relaxed, and he slowly walked to Anthony, as if wanting to apologize for his distrust. It was as though the dog were saying, "Let's talk this over now that all the weapons are down." The dog walked, tail tucked under his legs, never taking his eyes off of Anthony, until he was at the garage door.

Anthony was feeling panicky, as if someone were on to his plan and might blow the whistle at any moment. He truly had no idea how he was going to deal with Patches. Anthony walked into the garage, and Patches followed. Anthony sat down on the front bumper of his aunt's car—the trunk of which now held her lifeless body—and he looked sadly over to his oldest, most trusted playmate. "Whatsamatter, boy? Don't you trust me? Don't you remember all we've been through together? I would never hurt you, old boy. Never," and at that moment, Anthony was entirely sincere.

Patches, sensing his master's sincerity, walked over to him and licked his hands. Anthony smiled, not knowing how he could ever have considered bringing harm to his sweet, loyal hound. The dog sat, and Anthony massaged his furry head and neck, rubbing out the aches brought on by playing with a child less than half the dog's own age. Anthony gently massaged Patches, and thought of all the places they'd gone and the things they'd seen together, the adventures they'd had, and he wondered how much of it Patches recalled. He thought of Patches with such deep affection, and then he thought of Tobit, his dark lover that he now lived to please. Those days of ignorant, meaningless play with Patches were long in the past. The world was Tobit now.

Anthony soothed Patches' unsuspecting bones as if to say good-bye, and then he snapped the dog's tired, old neck with quick efficiency, and left him on the cold cement floor to leak out his bodily fluids in unavenged silence.

"This is too a grown-up minute," Christopher's voice rang out from the living room.

Anthony rushed back into the kitchen. "Sorry! You can come in now!"

As the child walked in eagerly, Anthony eyed the rat poison on the counter, then he turned to the open garage door. He realized that he didn't really know how long the poison would take to work, and it might even cause the boy to cry out. He couldn't risk arousing Eleanor's suspicion. "I think Patches is sick, Christopher. Would you go into the garage and try to wake him up?"

Christopher looked more serious than any adult Anthony had ever seen, as he marched out into the garage without a word to aid his loyal friend.

Anthony, looking after the boy and seeing his night's work nearing a close, found himself beginning to shake. There was a part of him that was screaming out against his every thought and action, but it was a Part of him that was easily smothered by his burning love and devotion for Tobit. He gathered himself and walked out to the garage, down the three cement steps, and towards the tool rack against the wall, directly behind Christopher.

"Wake up, Patches! Wake up! You shit yourself? Patches, please wake up!" Christopher's dim understanding of death was creeping in to his thoughts, and could be recognized in the quiver of his voice as he slowly turned his head and pleaded to Anthony with his large, watering eyes, "He won't get up! Anthony, please help me wake him up!"

Anthony had already removed the sharpened ax from its place on the wall, and as he stepped up to the child who was now frightened and bewildered by the death of his best and only friend, those desperate, trusting, six-year-old eyes seemed the perfect target for its shining, deadly blade.

*   *   *   *

Anthony at last arrived in the guest room. He was even amused by the fact that he and Eleanor, little known to her, had the house all to themselves, and if he made love to her as promised, they could be as loud as they liked. He smiled.

"What took you so long?" Eleanor sat up in bed, covering her naked breasts. She usually liked for Anthony to overpower her in bed. She liked for him to strip her clothes from her yearning body himself. Tonight, however, she felt it was better not to have anything in his way. She didn't want him to have the time to grow bored with her. "Is Christopher sleeping?"

Anthony smiled. "Out like a light." He looked at his wife, and he knew what she was expecting of him. He found himself frightened, because he felt nothing. There was no desire in his flesh—not for her.

Eleanor dropped the sheets, and she turned off the lamp at her bedside. Her ample breasts glowed in the moonlight. Just as Tobit had seemed to glow the night before, when he had smiled. The thought of Tobit caused Anthony's seemingly impotent organ to stir.

"Do you still love me, Anthony?"

The word love triggered only further thoughts of Tobit, and his maleness grew stiff, his flesh filled with desire—but not for her.

"I want you, Anthony. I want you to love me." Eleanor was pleading, as though she had seen the look of disinterest in his eyes. She had resigned herself to the fact that they would not make love after all. Then Anthony began to remove his clothing, without a word.

Anthony knew that he had to perform for his wife in order to keep her from growing suspicious, but he did not have to think of her. His thoughts, as he removed the last of his clothing, were of Tobit, and how he loved Tobit. He said nothing to his wife as he pulled away the sheets and mounted her brutally, like a loveless animal. As he pinned her to the bed with the weight of his muscular body, the warmth of her skin began to sicken him. As he rewarded her willingness with his rough and rhythmic thrusts, he was distracted by the perfume of her hair. She was nothing like Tobit. Nothing at all.

Anthony kept his eyes closed, and he pictured Tobit in warm surroundings to explain the warmth of Eleanor's sickening, woman's flesh. He imagined that Tobit had adorned himself with flowers, to explain the horrible, sweet smell of her hair. He thought of Tobit in the moonlight,

Tobit embracing him in the church, the glorious Chorus of Angels as Tobit held him locked in that euphoric kiss. Anthony thought of Tobit in the forest, and his thrusts grew faster and harder. He was grunting with the desire for a climax with only Tobit in his thoughts.

As Anthony quickened his violent pace, Eleanor was screaming with delight, having all but forgotten the sleeping child in the other room. She knew what was to come, as Anthony slammed into her with mounting ferocity, and she wanted to assure her place as his wife forever. "Don't pull out! Don't pull out!"

Anthony heard not a word she said as he continued to ravage her delicate body with his torrid and savage ramming. He moved faster and faster now with every second, as his body screamed towards climax. Thoughts of Tobit's passion and the blood-taste of his inhuman kisses held Anthony's thoughts without relent, until he at last spilled his pleasure into Eleanor's eager flower. And he thought of Tobit's delicious smile, Tobit's wonderful tears of joy.

Eleanor writhed beneath Anthony's hot and sweaty body as he finished, wanting to catch every last drop of his rarely-spent seed. She hoped and prayed that children would hold him to her. As he rolled off of her and fell to his side of the bed with heavy breaths, Eleanor thought that she had not been so satisfied, nor felt such affection from him in far too long. She smiled with delight at having had her paranoia washed away for all time. She sat up and kissed him, as he quickly drifted into sleep, and she saw his lips part to form a word, "Tobit..."

Eleanor's heart nearly burst, and she literally thought that it would. She sat for hours afterwards in shock, feeling raped and filthy—covered in the grime of his lust for another. Had Anthony been thinking of *him* the entire time! What if she had conceived, and the child was born of his lust for this *Tobit!* Eleanor was destroyed. Her mind could take no more...and then she remembered the knife.

Eleanor slowly crawled out of bed, so as not to wake the rapist at her side, and she walked over to the desk drawer in which she had hidden the blade. She quietly pulled open the drawer and removed the knife from its hiding spot. Knife in hand, she passed through the shadows like an assassin, crawling up beside Anthony in bed and placing the lethal blade at his throat. She could feel his pulse through the handle, and she wanted to stop it for all time. She hovered above him, and almost laughed out loud at his unsuspecting face as he slept deeply.

She thought about the lie that had been their "love-making," and how she had unwittingly taken such pleasure in it, when it had all been for this Tobit! She wanted to kill him. She intended to kill him. All it would take was the slightest bit of pressure, and he would get what he deserved. He was a liar and a rapist! He was unfaithful! He deserved to die!

Then Eleanor thought about the future, as though someone else had placed the thought in her head. What if she *had* conceived? What would she do without a husband? How would she survive? What if she went to prison?

In the end, the very last of Eleanor's reason won out. She took the knife away from Anthony's sleeping throat, and she slid it under her pillow as she lay down and thought frantically. *I can win him back. I can give him children...which Tobit can not. I can be more man than either of them!*

As the darkness of the night was taken by the light of dawn, Eleanor's conscious thoughts were taken by the darkness of her dreams.

5

"God no!" James awoke in panic from the most
horrifying dream he had ever known. He sat up
terrified, as if leaping away from the nightmare
itself. He took a few moments to catch his breath,
and to recall his unfamiliar surroundings. It took
him a moment to remember that he was not at
his own house. He had taken over the residency
for Father Maxwell, so that the older priest could
take a couple of weeks off and go to visit with his
sister in France. Actually, he had been more or less

forced to take some time off. It was hoped that he would return with a clearer mind, having been able to relax for a few days.

James found himself cold, due to the sweat that soaked his frightened body. He tried to forget the nightmare, but found it impossible. *Vampires!* He thought, *I'm up late at night frightened of vampires!* The concept would have made him laugh, had he not been so truly upset. He reached over to the side of the bed and picked up the phone. He dialed the number to his Aunt Betty's house, hoping that he would not be disturbing anyone's sleep—especially young Christopher's.

"Hello," came the soft, female voice from the other end.

"Eleanor?"

"Yes?"

"This is James. I'm sorry if I woke you or Christopher. I don't even know what time it is."

"James? You sound terrible! What's wrong?"

"Honestly, you'll probably call me an idiot. I've just been having nightmares, and I was wanting to talk to Big Brother about it."

Eleanor laughed. "I don't think you're an idiot, James. If anyone understands nightmares, it's Anthony. He's upstairs writing in his journal right now, and you don't know how adamant he was not to be disturbed. I'll have him call you right back, and I'll disturb him anyway if he's not done in ten minutes. He's been at it for a while now, and I'm ready for bed."

"I see."

"Oh, and don't worry about waking Christopher. Anthony tells me that Betty and Trixie came by this morning and picked him up."

"Is Aunt Betty home then?"

"No. She told Anthony that she'd still be gone a while. Anthony also told me that he thought we'd be gone ourselves before she returned."

James was puzzled. "That's so strange. Why are Aunt Betty and Trixie in hiding to discuss Christopher? You know Aunt Betty has never missed a funeral? She would normally have forced Trixie to go along to the funeral, and *then* they would tend to their other business. Something else must be going on that she hasn't told Anthony about. I think I'm worried. I wonder what it is."

"What I find odd is that they also took Patches."

"You're joking! Aunt Betty never takes Patches anywhere! Rarely even to the vet. And Trixie absolutely hates Patches, because he smells like a dog and gets hair on everything. This is almost too peculiar. Well, have Anthony call me back. I'm going to get up and make some hot cocoa, I think. It usually soothes my nerves."

"All right. I hope you feel better."

"Thanks. I love you."

Eleanor was taken off guard by the affectionate statement. She had barely been acquainted with her new brother-in-law for five days. "Yeah," she said. *It must be a preacher thing.* "I love you, too, James. Goodnight."

"Goodnight, Eleanor."

Eleanor hung up the phone and returned to her brooding. Anthony hadn't even said *I love you* when they had been in bed together the night before. He had said it before then, but she had somehow distrusted it. Thinking it over, he hadn't even kissed her while he was fucking her. She had come to the conclusion that there was no nicer word for what it had been, for it had certainly not been love making. She may as well have been his own sweaty fist for all the thought he had given to her. *Tobit.* Tears welled up, as she recalled the name he had spoken...when he had finished raping her.

Eleanor was so distraught. She felt so alone, now that everyone had gone. She had not seen James since the funeral, and his phone call had been the warmest moment of her day. *He loves me, and I didn't have to work for it at all.*

She had tried all day long to win Anthony's affection, and she had failed. She had done everything in her power to make him happy, within reason. She had cooked for him, said loving things to him, talked to him about the wonderful possibilities of their future together in Colorado. Perhaps it was time to step beyond the restrictive bonds of reason, for all of her attempts had failed. He loved Tobit—a man!

Anthony came down the stairs, having finished his writing. "Hey, El. Who was on the phone?"

Eleanor did not turn to face him. "James. He wants you to call him. He's at the church now, remember. Not at home. He was having bad dreams or something."

Anthony was deeply concerned. "They must have been pretty bad for him to call. But then, James has never been one for having nightmares anyway." Anthony went to the phone beside the couch and called his brother.

"Anthony?" the voice at the other end answered the phone hopefully.

"James! How are you?"

"I'm actually pretty shaken up. Did Eleanor tell you?"

"She said you'd had some bad dreams or something."

"Yeah. Actually, they were *really* bad. I know you're going to think this is crazy, but I really need to *see* you. I have to know that you're all right. I have to see it for myself. It was just one of those dreams."

Anthony was deeply worried. He had never heard his brother so upset. "James, that's not crazy. I'll be right there. Drink some cocoa."

"Already am."

"Good. I'll see you in a few minutes." Anthony then hung up the phone, not waiting for any formal sign-off from James. "I've gotta go to the church and see James. He's really shaken up. I'll be back later. Don't wait up."

"Why should I do that? You rarely come home before I fall asleep anyway." Eleanor paused, then went on bravely, still not turning to face him, "Are you having an affair?"

Anthony spoke too quickly, and without any sign of offense, "No. Eleanor, I would never, ever cheat on you. You know that. I have to go now. I'll be back." With that, Anthony left.

Eleanor sat on the couch, alone. She was lost in the web of lies, not knowing what to believe, not knowing how to think. She again thought of the knife she had hidden beneath her pillow. Then she thought of what it would take to become a man for Anthony. Somehow, she just couldn't keep the two thoughts apart. She couldn't decide if she wanted to please him...or to kill him.

*   *   *   *

Anthony approached the church urgently. He parked his car with much haste and made his way towards the front doors of the building. He stopped then, just before them, and he turned around, having sensed something. "Tobit." Anthony smiled with delight.

The tall form, garbed all in black, emerged from the shadows to greet him. "Hello, Anthony."

Anthony was very pleased to see his lover, for they had made no plans for their next meeting the night before. "Tobit! My beautiful angel! How clever of you to find me here tonight! I am very impressed! How do you do it?"

Tobit's face shined with pride at Anthony's words. "You are so wonderful, Anthony. You worship me and allow me to nurture you, and you nurture me as well." Tobit approached his young friend and kissed him deeply on the mouth. Then he pulled back, looking sorrowful. "I love you just as you love me." He looked away. "Perhaps more." He held Anthony's tender gaze with his sad, shimmering eyes. "You are here to see your brother?"

Anthony, knowing Tobit now so well, understood at once and shook his head with the warmest of smiles. "Tobit. *You* are my brother. Only you, my love. And I am yours."

Tobit was so surprised not to have to discuss this matter with Anthony. The young man was truly his, and perhaps not another word need be said. "Anthony, you amaze me!" Tobit smiled remarkably and kissed Anthony quickly on the lips. Anthony wanted it to go on, but Tobit stood back. "You must go to him now. Settle this matter. Tomorrow we will meet where we first met, and we will discuss the final preparations, and then we can be together forever. We will become the Bride and Groom."

Anthony embraced Tobit, and Tobit allowed it. They kissed with mounting passion, and then Tobit pulled away. "Go now, Anthony. Tomorrow, we will have all Eternity for our love." Tobit smiled, then faded almost magically back into the shadows.

Anthony stared off after him. "Beautiful, elegant, mystical Tobit. You are my brother. I will keep you ever at my side." He then turned and entered into the church—eager to sever all of his once brotherly ties to James.

*   *   *   *

James eagerly led Anthony into Father Maxwell's little apartment. He felt so relieved to have his older brother at his side. James led him to the tiny kitchen area and poured him some hot cocoa. Anthony smiled and took a seat at the little table. He took a sip, then jumped back from the extreme heat of it. Allowing his beverage to cool, Anthony let his eyes travel the little living area. There were so many religious paintings and carvings all around. Anthony thought that he Should not be surprised, considering who lived there. He was particularly taken, however, by the seeming excess of battle scenes between the angels Michael and Lucifer. Three paintings showed this violent scene of the devil being driven out by the archangel. There was a large stone sculpture at the side of the bed showing the same image, and a smaller one on top of the refrigerator.

Anthony then noticed a fourth painting hanging by the refrigerator, with beautiful writing blended perfectly to the scene. It was, Anthony thought, a very strange scene, and not quite so well matched with the words written with it. The painting showed the devil and his angels fleeing Pandemonium as Michael and his archangels seemed to be destroying it. Not a scene Anthony had ever seen anywhere. The words were an equally puzzling quote from Milton's *Paradise Lost*.

James noticed Anthony's studious fixation to the painting. "Father Maxwell painted that one himself a very long time ago. As far as I know, he's never painted anything but that. I suppose it's all he needed to paint. It speaks to his obsession."

"With angels?"

James nodded. "Mostly with Satan and the eternal struggle between good and evil. I never even realized how deep this devil thing went with him until he left, and he showed me around. I never come in here otherwise." James looked deeply troubled. "Maybe that's what's giving me nightmares. All these images of the devil and Hell." James spoke of this theory without conviction in his voice. It was obvious that he had other ideas as to why he had suffered nightmares.

Anthony was brought back to his original purpose at the mention of James' nightmares. "James, tell me about these dreams you had. What was so horrible about them that you had to see me in person in order to sleep again?"

James seemed very uncomfortable. "Anthony, you have to promise not to laugh."

"James, don't be ridiculous. Why would I laugh?"

"Well, sometimes I have dreams that are, well, different than others."

"What do you mean?"

"I mean, like, visions."

"What are you saying...like the *Virgin Mary* comes to you in the night and tells you about the future?" Anthony noticed that his tone was bordering on mockery, and he made a note to amend that when next he spoke.

James avoided Anthony's wondering eyes. "Well...not the Virgin Mary... actually."

"Who then?" Anthony had forgotten Tobit's wishes in the loving company of his brother James, and his only concern now was for his brother's mind.

James took a deep breath, then went on, "Well, sometimes it's Sally Field, dressed up like the flying nun...and other times, like this time, it's...Tori Amos."

Anthony could not believe his ears. His mouth was trembling as he struggled not to laugh. Finally the strain was just too much, and he burst out laughing, barely able to breathe.

James looked hurt. "What's so funny?"

"You!" Anthony continued to laugh. "This is the funniest stunt you've ever pulled, James! What makes it work is how straight-faced you are about it! Ha ha! The flying nun tells you all about the future!" Anthony was now giggling like a little girl, but the sternness of his sibling's face eventually made him stop. *Jesus Christ*, Anthony thought as a curse, *he's telling me the truth!* "I'm sorry, James. I was just...taken by surprise. That's all. Please go on. You saw Tori Amos..."

"No," James corrected him. "Anthony, please take me seriously. I very much need to tell you about this dream."

"All right. I'm sorry. Please go on."

James looked nervous still, but he seemed satisfied that his brother was willing to listen. "Okay. First of all, I didn't see her, I heard her. There was this scene...it was Hell, and there were vampires running around all over, and one of them was sucking out your blood. He looked like that photograph of Satan that Father Maxwell showed me before he left."

"Photograph of Satan?"

"Yes. I'll show it to you in a minute. It's ridiculous really. But back to my dream. Anyway, the vampire backs away from you, and you're a vampire too, and you start to eat this horrible hunk of flesh. Upon closer observation, I realize that this is Aunt Betty's severed head. This is when I find that I'm *part* of this scene, instead of just an observer. Her eyes open as you're biting into her, and she says, 'He's damned, James. You have to kill him! He's damned, and he's going to murder you!' This is when the other vampire, the one that was feeding on you, turns around and smiles at me. Then I start to hear that Tori Amos song in the background, but I can't tell where it's coming from. You know...that horrible song she wrote about God?"

The color had left Anthony's face at the mention of his lost Aunt Betty. "*Which* horrible song about God?"

"You know, that one that goes," James began to sing terribly, "God, sometimes you just don't come through. God, sometimes you just don't come through..."

"All right. I get the picture. Go on." Anthony was captivated, in spite of James' off-key lyrics.

"Well, that's when I ask the vampire, 'Who are you? What have you done to Anthony?' And he just smiles at me and starts to walk forward. All the while you're laughing and eating Aunt Betty's head, and Tori's still singing in the background. Then I shout at him, 'What is your name?'

"And he just says, 'My name is Damnation, and I drink of you deeply. My name is Damnation, and I drink of you deeply. My name is Damnation, and I drink of you deeply.' And he just keeps repeating this as he gets closer and closer, and I find myself unable to move—unable to break his spell.

"Then his teeth sink into my neck, and I can hear Aunt Betty screaming, 'No! No! No!' Then I hear Patches and Christopher vaguely in the background, but I don't see them, because everything goes black.

"That's when I woke up and opened my eyes. I didn't get up at first; I just looked around the room, relieved that it had just been a dream, but then I found myself trying to place what was different, because something clearly was, and I was still in too much of a stupor to recognize it right away. Then I realized what it was. I could still hear Tori, even though I was awake; and I know it wasn't the radio, because it was a different sounding version of the song. There was music, but no instruments. I can't explain it, but it was then that I knew I'd had a vision, and I sat up screaming in bed! That's when I called you."

Anthony had not blinked during the telling of his brother's tale. He thought of James' account of the music without instruments, and he recalled the Angelic Chorus that Tobit said was in every church and around all people of faith. The music that Tobit had allowed him to hear...with that delicious blood kiss. Anthony realized with panic that Tobit's spell had broken. He no longer wanted to kill James. He wanted to forget what he had done to the others he held dear. He rationalized, *A dream! I am still asleep and dreaming.* Anthony decided to turn the course of the nightmare by ignoring the past. He decided that he had not killed anyone, and he had never met Tobit. "James," he said, "that is the most fucked up shit I have ever heard!" He laughed, but the sound of it was hollow and without substance.

James could tell that it was a forced laugh, and that made him nervous. "Anthony, you're not dreaming."

Anthony looked horrified.

James looked away. "I don't know why I said that. It just sort of came to me, and it sounded like the right thing to say."

Anthony started trembling, whether from cold or fear James could not tell. He found himself not wanting to know. He made a quick attempt to redirect Anthony's thoughts. "Oh! Let me show you that so-called photograph of Satan that Father Maxwell showed me." James got up and went to the nightstand as Anthony watched him closely. Resting between the sculpture of Michael and Satan and a gold-plated letter-opener shaped like the Cross, there was an ancient looking photo, and James picked it up. "Remember how I told you that Father Maxwell claims to have met the devil when he was eighteen, but he rejected him and never forgot his face. Well, here's a picture of him standing with the man he firmly believes to have been Satan. I wonder what this guy could have done to him to make such a powerful impression." James tossed the photo to Anthony, and it landed on its face.

Anthony, still trembling slightly, read the back of the photo with dread. He noticed that the second name had been scratched out, and re-placed with another so that it read: *Me & The Devil — Delhi, India 1927*. Anthony turned it over in his hands. The picture was now almost seventy years old, it was tinted brown, with some colors carefully painted on, but the face and form of the man standing beside the young future priest was unmistakable. "Tobit!" Anthony dropped the photo and began to tremble uncontrollably.

James' voice was a whisper of shock, "How did you know his name? That's the name Father Maxwell told me he had crossed out. He said it was the name the devil had appointed to himself. Anthony, have you seen this man?"

Anthony's face contorted in such a way that James could see all the pain in his brother's heart. His mouth frowned horribly, and his eyes were forced to shut tight by his determined will to hold

142

back his tears, which spilled out just the same and covered his twisted face as, with great effort, he managed to nod his head.

James went to his brother and hugged him un- relentingly, and as he did so Anthony began to sob with the force of a horrified child. After sev- eral minutes, Anthony was able at last to speak through his sobs, and James sat back to see his face. "James, I'm so frightened! I don't know who I am anymore! I don't know who I am!" After this, his sobbing resumed, and James rose to hug his brother from behind and speak into his ear.

"It's all right, Anthony. It's all right. I'm go- ing to help you. It's going to be fine. We're in God's house now."

Anthony again remembered his night with Tobit in the sanctuary. *What does it mean to* Tobit *that we are in the house of God?* "Who is he, James? Do you know who he is? He won't tell me who he is...how old he is."

"I don't know, Anthony. You would know that better than I. What has he done to you?"

Anthony recalled the smothering of Aunt Bet- ty, he recalled the breaking of Patches' neck, the butchering of young Christopher...the abandon- ment of Christ... "Oh, James! It's all gone too far to turn back! I'm damned, James! I'm damned like your dream said!"

James went around to face his raving brother. "You're not damned, Anthony! I swear it! We can face this together, with God on our side! We can drive Tobit away, like Father Maxwell did."

Anthony looked hopeful. "That's right! How did he do it?"

"I don't know. He never told me more than that he rejected him. That's all you've got to do, Anthony. Just reject him."

"It's too late, James. God is not with me, and being in the church is no protection. Father Maxwell saw me in the church with Tobit three nights ago. That was me! Tobit is not afraid of the Church, and I have abandoned God! It was you, James! Your faith brought me out of his spell! Oh, James. I'm like a different person when I'm with him...nothing else matters when he's near me! I find I'll do anything to please him! I don't even think of Derek's death, and *he* killed Derek! It was him, and I love him anyway! You don't understand, James." Anthony seemed to calm down a bit. "You can't understand."

James was standing back from Anthony now, concerned, but frightened as well. "Why not? What can't I understand, Anthony?"

"I killed Aunt Betty! I killed Patches and Christopher! I became his murderer, and for love of him,

144

no matter how I love you, James...I'm going to do it...again. I know that I am. This is what I want."

"Anthony," James was clearly shaken. "Why do you have to do it again? Why can't you just turn your back on him?"

"Because I love him more than life! He's my savior. He's helped me to escape from all of my mistakes—all of my guilt and shame. I should never have married Eleanor...and Tobit can take me away from that. Tobit can take me away from everything! He's an angel to me!" Anthony stood, and James began to back up. "You broke the spell for me, James, only to show me how much I miss it. *He* is my brother, James. Tobit is my everything."

"Anthony, don't..." James' words were cut off by Anthony's fist, as the older brother punched him in the face. Then Anthony lunged forward and shoved his brother to the floor.

As James lay cradling his jaw, Anthony eyed the Cross-shaped letter-opener on the nightstand by the bed. He snatched it up and prepared to put it to deadly purpose, only to be greeted as he turned by James' fist in his face. James wasted no time, and he hit Anthony again, and again, and again, until Anthony fell to the floor.

James stood over his fallen brother. "Anthony, I hope you'll forgive me. I'm not going to let the devil have your soul. We're going to beat this! The power of Christ will triumph! I swear it." James was silent then, waiting for his words to sink in.

Anthony suddenly lifted his leg forcefully and kicked James violently in the testicles. James bent down in pain, and Anthony sprung up, punched him with all of his might, and forced him onto the floor. Then, holding James down under his own murderous weight, Anthony lifted the letter-opener over James' chest. "I love Tobit now," he said, "and nothing will ever keep us apart!" Anthony was in a rage as he brought the gold-plated dagger down into his brother's heart again and again—filled with unadulterated hatred for the man who had tried to turn him away from his dark lover.

6

Eleanor found herself alone again. Anthony had left this time without a word. He no longer felt he needed to explain his walks to her, and Eleanor hated that. His need to lie to her was the last connection she had to him, and she felt so alone. She wanted Betty to come back. She even missed the smell of Patches, and Christopher's endless questions and flirtations. Eleanor was now alone and at a complete loss. She felt that she had gone mad, or that she soon would, but there would be no one around to notice.

Over and over, her thoughts kept returning to Anthony's journal. The words he'd written had so wounded her before, that she had not dared open it again. Still, she wondered what insight could be gained from reading his more recent entries. Perhaps it would give her the edge she needed for winning him back.

After much thought on the matter, Eleanor rose from the couch that had become her only friend, and she ascended the stairs behind them.

Entering the bedroom, she noticed the journal was not on the desk. This only angered her, and she thought to herself that it would not be difficult to find. Anthony had not been terribly clever lately, in her opinion. She opened the desk drawer in which she had once hidden the knife that still rested beneath her pillow, and she was not surprised to see her husband's sinister journal—stupidly waiting there to be discovered.

She took the journal out and opened it on the little desk. She flipped quickly to his two latest entries, and she began to read.

August 18, 1995

I have learned so much about myself and the universe in these past two days. Yesterday was Derek's funeral, and Aunt Betty was unable to attend. I smothered her with a pillow the night before. It was the only way. I have to be with Tobit, and she was trying to come between us by nurturing me in his place.

Yesterday I broke Patches' neck and I also for all time silenced Christopher, because they seemed to need me far too much, and I have time now only to nurture my Tobit. I hid them all in the trunk of Aunt Betty's car. It's lucky for me that the last two were so small. I'm not worried about them being found, because I know that Tobit will take care of it...when we are at last together....

Eleanor stopped reading, and she turned violently away from the evil pages before her. She could not finish the entry. She was shaking, realizing how many holes had been in Anthony's stories about the family going off to discuss Christopher's future. James had pointed this out to her the night before.

James

Eleanor hadn't heard from her loving brother-in-law all day. Not since last night, when Anthony had gone to see him. She didn't know whether or not to believe the horrible things she had just read, and she didn't want to read anymore, because she was afraid of being convinced. She wanted to pick up the phone and see if James answered, but she was terrified of his possible failure to do so. She imagined that someone else would answer the phone. A stranger.

No, James isn't here. He had to leave suddenly to help decide who his six-year-old cousin should live with. He'll be back in a couple of days though...his brother told us this morning.

Eleanor did not want to hear it. She turned the pages to the very end of the latest entry: August 19. It was what Anthony had written just before he left. She skipped to the very last lines, wanting only to see what her husband had most recently written:

And so, I go now to be with Tobit. He has become my Christ, my nurturer and my brother, the only one I love and care for. He has promised that tonight, after one last bit of preparation, we will be together forever. We will be the Bride and Groom. And nothing will ever stand between us.

150

Eleanor closed the book in utter despair. What was there to do? She had to know whether the journal were true, for if it was, Anthony would almost certainly murder her as well. How else could he and Tobit be *the Bride and Groom*?

Why won't he talk to me? I can be his groom! I can be just as good as any man!

Eleanor looked over at the pillow as tears streamed down her face. She got up from the desk and uncovered her hidden knife. She studied the deadly blade, as she ran her fingers through her long, feminine red hair. Then, with suddenness, she realized that she could be getting upset for nothing. She had no evidence that her lying husband had written a single word of truth. It could all be an elaborate fantasy. *I hid them all in the trunk of Aunt Betty's car.* There was one way she knew that she could be certain. If there were three corpses in the trunk of that car, then she knew there would be no point in calling James for help.

Clutching the kitchen knife as though it were a sacred object, Eleanor left the guest room and moved to learn the truth.

*　　*　　*　　*

The car keys were hung in the kitchen, right beside the garage door. She timidly grabbed them with her free hand, and she held them as she looked at the door. She didn't really want to know what was in that trunk, but she felt she had to see. After what seemed an eternity, Eleanor opened the door, and she walked into the garage.

The stench within was terrible, and Eleanor feared the worst. She noticed the giant, brown stain on the floor, and her steps towards the rear of the car grew smaller.

When she at last made her way to the trunk, she paused just as she had at the garage door. She was sobbing with fear—and hatred of that fear. She prayed to God that there would be nothing in the trunk, and the nightmare would end. If the trunk was empty, she felt that she could sleep without fear for the rest of her life. Shaking as her hands were, Eleanor found it difficult to fit the key to its lock, but she managed just the same. She turned it, jumped back at the loud pop of the lock, and then the trunk rose up...and there they were.

Eleanor screamed the most horrified scream that she had ever known. She screamed with such force that it surprised her to see the garage windows had not been shattered...as her sanity had been. She finally gained enough control over herself to look into the trunk again. She reached in, not knowing why herself, and she lifted Patches' rank remains. "Patches. Come on. You're a good boy, aren't you? You can help me, right? Like Lassie! Lassie, come home." Eleanor, in her madness, began to giggle without any amusement at all. It was simply the only emotional reaction she had left.

She lifted the dog completely out of the trunk, and she dropped it in horror, screaming even more ferociously, as she witnessed the state of Christopher's butchered body. She reached up instantly and slammed the trunk closed. She then stood, shaking so fiercely that she thought she would explode. She fell down beside the dead, old dog, and she snuggled up with it, as though it were a Teddy bear. She sobbed into the creature's dead fur, "Lassie come *home!*"

She felt her long hair once again, she thought of her husband and became aware of the knife that had still not left her terrified hand. *My husband needs a man,* she thought, *and he deserves to die.*

*   *   *   *

Anthony walked through the doors of David and Jonathan's, for the third time in his life, to find it busier than ever before. There was once again an Erasure song playing over the speakers, and Anthony found it entirely appropriate. The words seemed to accent the moment, when he glanced across the room and once again locked eyes with his beautiful Tobit.

Anthony made his way across the room, and Tobit rose from his barstool to meet him half way. The two men hugged each other within the crowd of Saturday night patrons. Anthony flashed a smile at Tobit and looked at one of the speakers. "'I Love Saturday'"

"Yes," Tobit commented. "So do I."

Anthony laughed. "That's the name of the song. I love you, Tobit."

The taller man smiled with boyish charm. "I know. I love you too. Are you ready? Are you sure that you still want for us to be united for all time?"

Anthony rolled his eyes in mock-disgust, clearly amused. "Tobit, you know that I do. I belong to you, and you have become my only joy! I want us to be united more than anything."

Tobit spared a glance to either side of them. "We're starting to attract attention. We should leave now."

"Very well, my love." Anthony took Tobit's hand in his, and the two men forced their way through the crowd.

"I like this song," said Tobit. "It seems so fitting, and it's so happy."

"Yes," Anthony agreed. "Just like us." He opened the door and listened to the song, as he bid his farewell to the bar for the night. And as he heard the song's closing lyrics, he thought that surely the song had not been entirely prophetic; for, while it was happy and upbeat, singing the praises of love, it ended with the bitter question of whether the lovers had been in denial of the fact that they were bound to fall apart. As the doors closed behind them, the two fiends went out into the waiting summer night.

*   *   *   *

Eleanor had returned to the upstairs guest room with Patches. She sat at the little vanity just beside the bathroom, petting Patches' lifeless fur as he rested on the counter. She stared into the mirror, unblinking, and she studied herself. The woman that she was. She hated herself and wanted to die. "He'll see, Patches. He'll see." She looked back to the knife that had still not left her hand. "We'll show him what he's missing in the man that I can be...and then he'll have to die." She grinned with a skeleton's smile, as a single tear drop fell from her wide and vacant eyes.

*　　*　　*　　*

Anthony and Tobit stood outside, not too far from David and Jonathan's. Anthony was still humming the tune that had ushered them from the bar, and his ability to stay on key was little better than James' had been. Tobit laughed at him with great affection. "Anthony, you sing like a..."

Anthony smiled gleefully up at Tobit. "Like a what?"

"Like a dove," Tobit lied.

Anthony was glowing with joy. "Tobit."

"Yes, Anthony?"

"Tell me now. What remains to be done so that we may be together? I have already assured you that it is only you to whom I pledge my worship, my affection, my vulnerability and my brotherhood. What other assurance must you have, before you'll have me in full?"

Tobit was visibly pleased by Anthony's eagerness. "I am surprised that you do not already know, for what else could I need to see? Who is your bride, Anthony? That is the only thing I still must know. When you have shown me that *I* am your bride, and I alone, then we will be together in full for all time, and nothing will ever come between us."

Anthony suddenly looked somber. "Eleanor..." *Eleanor who nurtures me, Eleanor who I nurture in return, Eleanor who is always faithful at my side, Eleanor who I so worshipped on our wedding night...*He looked Tobit in the eyes. "Will you offer no assurances in return, Tobit? Why do you never tell me anything of yourself?" Tobit looked away sadly, and Anthony remembered the photo he had seen the night before. "I can no longer believe that you are in any way human. I saw a photograph of you that was sixty-eight years old, and yet you appear younger than myself. You cast such a spell over me with those deep and beautiful eyes. The words you speak intoxicate me. I must know who you are. Tell me who you are!"

Tobit met Anthony's glare reluctantly. "I am Tobit..."

"No!" Anthony was becoming angry. "I don't mean your name. *What* are you, Tobit? You are not an ordinary man! You claim to be as old as temptation. You have a power over me that I would trade for nothing! What are you? Are you a demon? An angel? Some sort of god-like space alien? What? I *must* know! If we are to be together always, I must know, Tobit. I love you, and I simply want to know what it means to be a part of you." Anthony began to weep with desperation. "What does it mean to have you as my bride?"

Tobit wept as well—unable to stand the tone of Anthony's angry voice. "Please don't hate me, Anthony. I will tell you what I am tonight. I will tell you what and who I am all at once. But I must be assured. When you have assured me that you want only me as your bride, I will find you instantly, and I will reveal the truth to you. I will tell you who I am, and you will understand what it means to court me...and to have me as your bride for all eternity."

Anthony seemed contented. "I would never hate you, Tobit. You are my one love. You are my bride." Anthony made as though to kiss Tobit, but the taller man stopped him and shook his head sorrowfully. "No, Anthony. This is our night. We must wait until it's done. Give me this final assurance, and my kisses will be yours forever."

Anthony nodded his head. "Yes. There is nothing that I will not do for you, Tobit." He looked into the distance. He looked towards the home of his late Aunt Betty, and he wondered after his lovely Eleanor—his soon departing bride.

*　　*　　*　　*

Anthony walked into the house through the back door. He was startled by the darkness, and when his eyes had adjusted, he was startled again by the open garage door and the absence of the keys that normally hung beside it. He looked around, his heart beating swiftly. He was sure that someone had discovered his lies, and who was there save Eleanor? Anthony closed the door behind him, and he took two nervous steps forward. His shoes seemed to click on the floor with unnatural loudness. "Eleanor? Are you here?" He was startled by the cackling, banshee-like laughter that answered his call. He was not at all sure that it *was* Eleanor. "Eleanor? Where are you? I must see you!"

She called to him in an eerie, distant-sounding voice, "We're coming, Anthony! And I hope you're pleased with what we've done."

Anthony was confused. "We?" Anthony began to tremble slightly at the feeling in the air, as he listened to her gentle footsteps descending the carpeted stairs.

Eleanor came into view at last, and she stood just within the kitchen doorway. "Are you happy now, Anthony? Is this what you wanted?"

Anthony gasped out loud in utter horror. There stood a tasteless mockery of his once adorable Eleanor. She stood there, glaring at him with mindless eyes. She wore the very suit and tie that he himself had worn to Derek's funeral two days before. Her hair was all but gone. Her once elegant, curling red locks had been brutally hacked from her head, leaving her with the appearance of having been afflicted with mange. She showed her teeth as though she were a wild jungle cat eyeing a potential prey. And under her left arm was Patches. Lifeless, reeking Patches. His sunken eyes were open still, and though they had no shine of life at all, Anthony cringed from their loveless and accusing stare.

Tears fell from Eleanor's screaming, mad eyes. "What's the matter, Anthony? Why are you looking at me like that?" She groaned horribly. "I thought

this is what you wanted! I thought...I thought..."
She suddenly screamed the most hellish cry from
the very tops of her lungs, "*I can bend you over just
as well as* he *can!*" She groaned violently and
removed a lighter from her pocket. Before Anthony
could even wonder why, she lit the rotting dog on
fire and hurled it directly at him as she screamed,
"Die! Bastard! Die!"

Anthony was amazed at how quickly the cadav-
er went up in flames, and he was in absolute
terror as it came flying towards him like a
vengeful spirit straight out of Hell. In the instant before Anthony dodged out of the way, he
found himself looking directly into the old dog's
black and lifeless eyes.

Anthony was more afraid than he had ever
been in his life. However, he found himself uncertain of the cause. Was he afraid of his mad and
dangerous wife, or was he afraid of himself for
having driven her to such a state? Was he afraid of
the guilt he'd found in Patches' murdered eyes?
He turned to see that Patches' body had caught
the wall behind him on fire with amazing swift-
ness. The fire seemed to spread then like a living
thing—ravenous as it sought to consume the home
of his youth.

Anthony saw that Eleanor was gone. He called
her name in a trembling voice, "Eleanor?" He was

once again answered by a witch-like cackle and a banshee's wail. He backed over to a drawer, just before it too was taken by the flames of Patches' vengeance, and he grabbed the sharpest knife within. He then slowly crept to the stairs, and he followed the trail of butchered red hair that led him to the guest room.

Anthony had wondered why there was not a light on in the house, but now he felt sure that it was all a part of Eleanor's death trap. She knew the truth, and now she meant to keep him from ever being with Tobit. She would kill him before losing him to the better man. And perhaps it was Anthony's guilt that kept him from turning on the lights himself.

He walked into the room in which he and Eleanor had last been Bride and Groom, and he saw no sign of her in the secretive shadows of the night. The moon's light shined through the window, and he went to it, as though it had beckoned him. "Eleanor, where are you?"

The shrill scream that answered him carried no words, only hatred from the purest and most scalding depths of Hell. She too had a knife in hand, and she ran into the room, clumps of hair still flying from her scalp like the pieces of a decaying corpse. She swung her knife at him with unyielding determination three times before he grabbed her, dropping his own blade to the ground to do so. She screamed again and bit him with the full force of her raging jaws. Anthony shouted out in pain and let her go.

As he took the careless time to examine his deep and jagged wound, Eleanor laughed like a villainess from the darkest of fairy tales. He met her eyes, and her laughter died instantly. She glared at him, her bloody teeth bared, and she growled like a panther as she lunged at him with all her might— her shining blade glistening in the moonlight.

Anthony leapt out of her path at the absolute last second before the knife would have sliced into his chest. Eleanor's momentum proving too much to stop, her knife prepared her way as it broke the glass, and she followed with a crash. Eleanor plummeted with a blood-curdling scream from the high, second-story window. However, the sounds that Anthony found even more the horror were the slap-thud of her frail form hitting the ground and the terrible silence that followed.

Trembling and weeping with fear and shock, Anthony made his way to the shattered window, and he looked down to see her broken body breathless on the ground. The blood that poured from beneath her, and from her upper back as well, led Anthony to believe that she had landed on her own blade. There was no hope in his heart that she had managed to survive, and he began to sob with that realization. He had not killed her himself in actuality, but he had driven her to the madness that had killed her in his name.

Anthony realized with even further horror that he was *feeling* such incredible guilt and self-loathing. Tobit's spell was broken again, and he now craved it like a drug. He yearned for nothing more than that spell that could hide him from his guilt. As it was now, his regret was driving him. He had to go to Eleanor.

Anthony ran down the stairs and fought his way through the now unstoppable flames. He shot through the smoldering back door, and he stumbled to Eleanor's lifeless side.

He sat on his knees beside her, in the growing pool of her crimson blood. He saw that he had been right, as the metallic tip of her well-sharpened blade was quite visibly peeking through her blood-drenched back.

Anthony sobbed aloud. "Why? Oh, God! Oh, Eleanor, please! Oh, why? What have I done? What have I done?"

Anthony's eyes caught the movement of Tobit, as the much older man seemed to pass through the bushes as though they were air. Tobit said nothing. He simply watched.

"Tobit!" Anthony was desperate. "Please, my love! I can't feel your spell! Please! I can't bear this pain! You must take me from this pain!"

Tobit was unsmiling, as he spoke icily, "No."

Anthony was stricken. "What? Why? Please, Tobit! Mystify me as you always have! Make me forget my evil deeds!"

"No, Anthony. That game has ended. Now *I* am your bride...for all time. I only mystified you so that you would complete your vows to me. And now it is done. This pain is yours. You have earned it well. And it will follow you throughout the many centuries that you must now endure."

"You can't be serious! I never meant to...I thought...I didn't..."

"Yes, Anthony. You did. You chose this. My spell did leave you many times, and you came running back, unable to face your sins."

"Dear God."

"Vain words. He will not hear you now. *I* am your god, as you chose me. It is the folly of this era to glamorize and romanticize monsters. I tell you truly, Anthony. A monster is a monster—never more, never less. When you succumbed to me, you became like me. If I am a monster, then so must you be."

Anthony spoke painfully through his streaming tears, "What are you? Please, tell me that much, Tobit. Monster. Tell me who and what you are!"

"I am he who has called to you and all men from childhood on. I am the tempting voice that hides in fear and lust. You have courted me since the day you were born. Your fate was visibly sealed when you chose to live a lie, but you had coveted my hand even long before then."

Anthony had not the mind now to ponder the meaning of Tobit's words. He wanted a simple answer, and it seemed there was none to be had. He looked in torment at his shattered Eleanor. "I am damned—without hope." He shook his head with deadly resignation. "I have become my own damnation."

Tobit shook his head, and a cold and loveless smile crept into his lips. "No, Anthony." Tobit began to walk closer to his disillusioned lover, and he parted his lips, revealing his dagger-sharp teeth in the smile of a cobra just before it strikes. "*I* am your Damnation, and I now drink of you—deeply."

CHRISTIAN'S DILEMMA

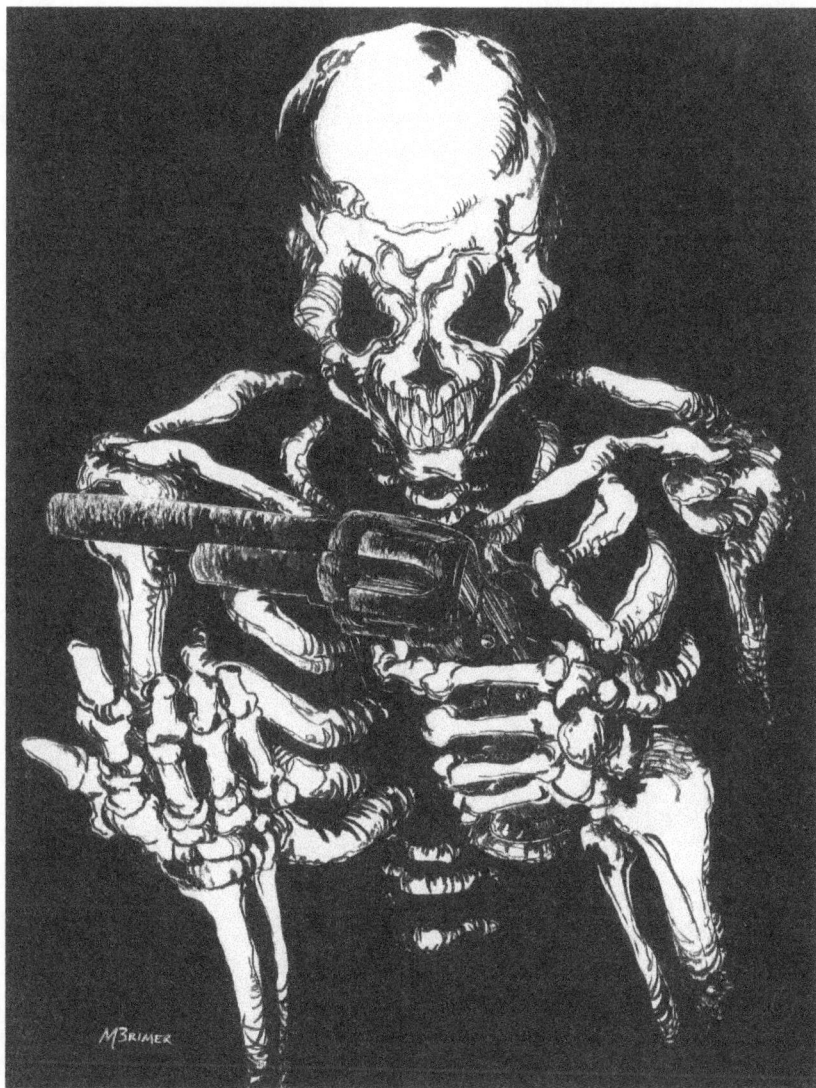

"I do not believe what the shepherd says; that the master is not pleased with me; that the master will not have me. If that were true, then why would I even be here to begin with? Was it not the master himself who added me to his flock in the beginning?"

— The Rainbow-Colored Sheep

Christian opened his bedroom door and looked out into the living room. His heart seemed to freeze as he caught sight of the closet door beside the front entrance of his small apartment. He took a deep breath, attempting to swallow whole his great trepidation. He stepped out of his room. "Not this time. This time I will finally see what's supposed to be there."

Winter had come to Dallas, Texas a week before, which, as Christian himself was well aware, meant that the winter was already half over. Such was the weather in Dallas. What troubled Christian, however, was not the nonsense weather of Texas; rather it was the fact that winter was likely half over, and he had not yet been able to retrieve his winter jacket from the entryway closet. There was something in the closet that was not supposed to be there. Something frightening. Something which even now had the young man questioning everything.

Christian closed his eyes and said a silent prayer. He then glared at the closet and decided to march right at it and take his jacket with God's aid. Surely he had imagined it all those times before. Surely there was nothing in the closet save for his jacket, the vacuum cleaner, various board games, and shoe boxes full of knickknacks. Ignoring his fear, Christian followed through with his plan. He marched right up to the closet, threw open the door...and froze in his tracks, completely forgetting his frail courage from the moment before.

This was no closet. A fierce, cold wind issued from the cavern before him, accompanied by wailing, screaming, and a thousand more terrible sounds of agony. There was blackness so deep, tinted only by the red light of flames, glinting off the stony cave walls, which must have been burning deep within the cavern. "Why can't this be Narnia in my closet?" Christian asked aloud, not knowing if even God was there to hear him. He heard the now too familiar clicking and rattling of bones on the stone floor. He knew it was coming, but he could not bring himself to move. He needed to ask it just one more time.

The villain appeared. A human skeleton, held together by evil itself, walking about as though it were a living thing. It stood there in the doorway, mere inches from where the young man stood. "Ah, Christian! I'm glad you've come back."

Christian felt tears welling up in his eyes. Tears of anger and frustration. Tears of hatred for himself, because he was so afraid. He managed to speak through his fear, "Why do you always pretend to be so surprised?"

The skeleton shrugged, red light dimly filling its hollow eye sockets like laughter. "Because you're pathetic. You're a coward. I figured you would have given up by now. You know, Christian, everything will be so much easier on all of us if you'll just come on in. I know it's cold, but let's face facts. You're cold where you are." The skeleton cackled.

Christian trembled, as a tear ran down his pale cheek. "Please, sir. Give me back my jacket. That's all I'm asking for. Keep everything else. I just don't want to be cold anymore. I'll never bother you again. You can have the closet for all I care."

The fleshless fiend cackled some more. "You humans are all alike! What makes you think you can negotiate?" The skeleton lifted a cigar to its lipless teeth and took a puff. "Get this through your head, boy: you have nothing to live for. The church has rejected you, and therefore so has God. Your soul is a waste. No one really loves you. You are just an irritant to everyone. Don't you see it? Everything you do, every thought, every breath is a sin. just come along nicely, my pretty sinner. We've got your room all done up for you. You'll have eternal torment here, but at least you won't have bills to pay. It's cold, again I know, but your jacket's in here somewhere."

"Why do you say such terrible things? Why are you tormenting me, of all men, why me?"

"I say these things because they are true. You are a horrible person, Christian. An abomination. A sinner. An unforgivable soul. Your friends would never let on that they thought so. Why should they? It would make them feel guilty to ever tell you the truth." The skeleton inhaled again on the cigar and blew out a great cloud in Christian's tear-streaked face. "You were created evil, man! Just turn to the Bible, go to your church if you don't believe me. Creatures of your like are damned, all. There is no salvation, and in the meantime you are wasting everybody else's air. Stop breathing. Stop bothering all these people you claim to love that hate you so. Stop pretending that even God loves you. Stop!" The thing held up a pistol in its left hand. "Don't open this door again until you've made up your mind to use this."

Staring into those lifeless sockets, Christian reached up and took the gun from the skeleton's hand.

"We loaded it full and polished it just for you, Christian. Now come home, where we will treat you as you deserve to be treated. We will spare you all the lies about love which have fooled you for so long. You are hated where you are. You know this." A skeletal arm reached out and latched onto the doorknob. "Remember, boy. It only takes one shot."

The door slammed shut, and Christian fell to the floor, frozen to the soul. He wept and stammered to himself, "I just want my jacket back. God shield me from the cold." And he remembered the skeleton's words. *Stop pretending that even God loves you.* Then Christian only wept.

*   *   *   *

After twenty minutes or so of suffering there on the floor, Christian reached a decision. The monster in the closet was right. The world had turned on him. How could anyone love such a loathsome creature as himself? He was a fiend. He stood against all that was holy. His friends must have been lying to him for years about their affection; for what had he ever done but burden them?

Christian sat up and collected himself. He felt somewhat refreshed after shedding his tears. He usually did. He noticed a draft coming from the crack of the front door. He smelled the winter air, as though to savor it for the last time. He felt the heavy gun in his hand, and he looked at it. No. He realized that he would need some mental lubrication before he could pull the trigger. Christian hadn't been drunk in seven years, but at this point he could think of no better way to leave the world than while not really comprehending it.

Christian stood and opened the front door. The chilling winter air greeted him, mingled with the strangest sound. It was melodic, but strangled and akin to despair. Like someone was weeping musically. Christian shook his head and stepped out to meet his final outing, then he stumbled over something so large that even as he fell he did not know how he had missed it.

Christian twisted around in mid descent, managing to hit the cement porch with his feet and rump all at once. "Rats!" He wanted to shout out again as the uncomfortable throbbing of his rear end urged him on, but he was distracted by the sight of what he'd tripped over. "What the...?"

There was a stranger, huddled there on Christian's porch, sobbing. The stranger was dressed all in white robes and had long, silken white hair that covered his face as he wept. And what a sound was this weeping; so melodic it seemed that Christian found himself wanting to capture the tune of it; he wished he could join in with the stranger and make harmony with that wonderful sound. "Excuse me," Christian ventured at last. "I didn't mean to uh...well, trip...over you." He thought for a moment. "What are you doing sobbing on my porch anyway? What's your name?"

The stranger sat up and wiped the tears from his eyes. Eyes, Christian noticed, that sparkled with life like two blue planets drifting in a universe of serenity. The stranger's face was flawless, his skin seemed softer than down. And when he spoke, his voice was the very sound of love, "Oh, I'm sorry. My name is Lokiel. I'm crying here on your porch, because I can't stand to see you in so much pain, Christian. I can't stand it that you won't let me help you."

Christian's eyes went wide. Was this a compatriot of the skeleton? Had the monster left the closet to help him pull the trigger?

"No, young friend! Not like that! Not at all! I'm batting for the other team. Understand?"

Christian shook his head, dazed and afraid.

The stranger then rose to his feet and punctuated his remarkable presence by unfurling great, beautiful white wings from his shoulders. The feathers seemed to dance, as they shimmered like crystals in the sunlight. "I'm an angel. Your guardian."

Christian shook his head, not sure what to say. He finally composed himself and felt anger taking the stand. "My guardian angel? Then where have you been until now?"

The angel looked sad. "We've been with you all along, Christian. All along."

"We?"

"Yes, the four of us. Myself, your other two guardians, and of course God. God is everywhere."

"I have three guardian angels? Then where are the other two?"

"Well," Lokiel answered, "the way it works is that everyone has at least three guardian angels, and every guardian angel is assigned to at least three people. And this brings us to the other reason for my tears. Your other two guardians are both on call to one of their other charges. This is the first time in your twenty-six years that I've ever been left completely alone with you, and now you're off to kill yourself." The angel's voice caught in his throat, and he again began to weep. "I've failed you, Christian. I've failed. Why must you hate yourself so?"

Christian was flabbergasted. Indeed, where *had* these angels been throughout his ordeal with the skeleton? Remembering the absence of his jacket, Christian felt the cold and began to shiver. He stood up and reached past the angel, closing the front door. Then he spoke sternly, "Look, Loko...Loopy...uh..."

"Lokiel!"

"Yeah, yeah. Lokiel, Gabriel, Clarence...whatever! I really can't understand any of this right now. There's been this thing in my closet for I don't know how long, it won't let me have my jacket, I can't afford a new one, and I just realized what a useless person I am. You're telling me that I've had not just one, but three guardian angels all along, and not once did *any* of you make an effort to help me. And now you're crying, showing yourself to me only after you feel that you've failed me? Thanks a lot. I guess God really does hate me. The skeleton was right."

Lokiel let out a terrific sob, "No! You've gotten us all wrong, Christian!"

"Stop crying," Christian barked in irritation. "Figures I'd have an overly emotional, melodramatic pansy for a guardian angel."

The angel looked stricken, and his eyes squinted in a vain effort to hold back even more tears. "Oh, Christian. You shouldn't say such things. I love you so much. We all do." Lokiel continued his sobbing.

Christian couldn't help but feel guilty about hurting the beautiful creature. He tried to soften his mood. "Hey, Lokiel. I'm sorry. I'm just lashing out. I'm just at the end of my wits, and I've been afraid for so long..." The anger threatened to break back through the surface, but Christian pushed it down. Suddenly collected and aware of his surroundings, Christian began again to shiver in the cold. "Look, if you want to try and help me understand, you're welcome to come along."

The angel's weeping stopped, and he came to full attention, looking as excited as a puppy whose master had just come home. "Oh, but, Christian! Where are we going?"

Christian shrugged. "I don't know. The Inwood Tavern? J. R.'s? Just somewhere that I can get good and drunk before I pull the trigger."

Lokiel looked nervous, though still excited. "But, Christian! You don't drink!"

The human held out his arms. "Well, I don't commit suicide either, Lokiel. Might as well do both on the same day, right? Just look at it this way: in either case, at least I won't be forming a habit." Christian laughed, and Lokiel could not help but laugh along with him. It was a good sign to see the man laughing, even at the thought of something as morbid as his own self-destruction.

The pair began the quick descent on the stairs from Christian's second-story apartment's porch to the sidewalk below. Suddenly, Lokiel paused. "Christian?"

The man turned his head to regard the angel over his shoulder. "Yeah?"

"Why must we go to a bar?"

Christian turned around in full to glare at the angel. "Because," he held up the gun in his right hand, "I can't very well take care of things when I'm in my right mind. I need to dull my senses."

Lokiel spoke nervously, "Well...it just doesn't seem fair that the skeleton gets to talk to you when you're sober, but I can't present my arguments until you're drunk. Besides," he shrugged, "they usually don't serve my kind at bars."

Christian let out a long frustrated sigh, then motioned for the angel to go back up the stairs. "Okay. We'll talk on the porch, in the cold. I suppose I'll suffer for you just as I've suffered for the other. Guess you're right; they wouldn't serve an angel at a bar. Too hard to accommodate. Most places I've been don't have much in the way of manna muffins or ambrosia wine."

The angel, now at the top of the stairs and taking a seat in one of the two plastic chairs on Christian's porch, giggled gleefully. "Oh, Christian, you're so witty! That's one of the things we so love about you. Here you are entertaining the most horrible ideas, blackly depressed, and yet you still make a joke!" Lokiel fixed Christian with a glowing, pearl-white smile. "I love so much the man that you are. I want to hug you, hold you, kiss you on the cheeks and on the forehead..."

Christian stood now at the top of the stairs, all the shadows of his soul fully visible in the expression of his face. "But not on the lips. No." He shook his head, as he reluctantly took the chair beside the angel. "That would be too wicked. That would be a sin." He met the angel's sad, blue eyes with his own.

Lokiel saw that their dialogue had at last begun. Christian was asking him all the questions that tormented his heart with that pleading, desperate gaze. It was time to do all within his power to turn this man around. As always, however, and to Lokiel's deep frustration, humans had been given the great gift of free will. Lokiel could not simply change Christian's way of seeing himself. He couldn't simply stop Christian from doing harm to himself. These things could only be done by Christian himself. All Lokiel could do was discuss it with him, and the man would be left to make up his own mind. All Lokiel could do was guide him and love him.

Lokiel took a moment of luxury, in which he soaked up the beauty of this uncertain man. How beautiful were these creatures of free will to the Almighty and all of His acolytes. Yet none of them could see it for themselves. Lokiel wished that he could simply show Christian how the creatures of Heaven perceived him—lovelier than the most exotic flower; for all flowers lived and breathed as humans did, but never did they deviate from the course laid out for them at the beginning of all things. They grew from seeds, became flowers, bloomed in their season, died in their time without argument. Humans were born and grew, but what they became was always a surprise. Humans bloomed and died as flowers did, but never without a fight, internal or otherwise. Humans struggled with their destinies, matters of life and death; humans questioned everything. Humans lived and breathed, just as flowers did, and yet they did so with such passion and mystery, such sound and fury. No angel had ever seen a flower, nor a sunset rich with all the colors of Creation, that came forth with even half the beauty of a human man or woman caught up in the endless struggle of making either a simple or daring choice.

Lokiel spoke, "Christian, no. Kissing you on the lips would not be a sin in itself...but, it would be wrong for me to mislead you. It would be wrong, for what a kiss on the lips suggests in your culture. It would be too easy for you to fall in love with me. Humans can't help but fall in love with angels that caress them in a human fashion, and...truth to tell...angels can fall in love with humans just as quickly. It's a dangerous thing, and so we are told to keep a certain distance. Rarely do we manifest ourselves before human eyes. Only at the end...or in emergencies. Emergencies such as this."

Christian continued to drink in the beauty of Lokiel as the angel spoke. He knew that it was truth he'd heard, for surely it would not take much to infect him with such love for this luminous, compassionate creature sitting beside him. But that had not been the meaning of his comment, and he suspected Lokiel knew as much, for the angel had read his mind just a moment before. He looked down to his knees, and a silent tear rolled down his cheek, leaving a stinging trail of coldness behind it in the winter air.

"Christian, do you know how beautiful you are?" Lokiel asked. "How can you possibly think that you are unloved? How can you possibly think that God would not have you?"

Christian looked back to the angel, a flash of anger in his stare. "How can you possibly think otherwise?"

Lokiel looked as though he would weep again, but, to Christian's surprise, the emotional angel held its composure. "Christian, you must speak to me. Of course I know your thoughts, but they are so chaotic at times. They contradict each other as a rule. You must speak your thoughts, Christian. You must question out loud. Until you voice a thought, you have never truly faced it. This is true for all thinking creatures. You must speak or act before your thoughts can be your truth. Tell me, Christian, why do you see yourself as so loathsome to God's eyes? How has this demon convinced you?"

Christian pondered the words of the angel. It seemed right, the things Lokiel said. Then again, so had the words of the demon skeleton who'd preached its hatred so convincingly. Even as he thought on the matter, Christian could recognize the conflict of his thoughts which Lokiel had pointed out. "Well, for one thing," he looked to the clouds, "I have no love for the Church. At times, I even go so far as to hate it. The hypocrisy of it. The judgments it hands out to us so mindlessly." Christian reflected for a moment. "Yes," he said at last. "I do hate the Church. I hate it with a devil's passion."

"And yet," Lokiel added, "you continue to teach Sunday school for the young people every week, without fail. You continue to go there."

Christian regarded the angel in utter confusion. "Yes, I do. Why? I don't know. Perhaps I'm a hypocrite myself. For that, if nothing else, I deserve to die. What use to the world is a hypocrite who hates hypocrites? Indeed I am the epitome of hypocrisy."

Lokiel began to giggle again, and he covered his beaming smile with both hands.

"What?" Christian asked crossly.

"Forgive me," Lokiel said, as his giggling wound down. "You sound funny to me. All your thoughts are trying to break through, and you say the most hilarious things. I love you for it, even if you do think yourself the hypocrite of hypocrites."

"Well, I'm glad you find my self-hatred so amusing."

"Oh, Christian! It's not that at all! For I see the thoughts which haven't come out of you yet. I see, in fact, that you are not a hypocrite at all." Lokiel smiled. "Don't you see it? You do know why you go. There is a reason that you teach Sunday school in spite of your hatred of the Church. Tell me now. Why do you do it, Christian?" He continued to smile lovingly, as he repeated the question, "Why?"

Christian considered the question in silence, until he found the answer. There was fire in his eyes when he again looked to Lokiel and spoke, "It's a defiant thing, really. I hate the Church, but I love those people. I suppose I hate the Church, because it would judge them too harshly. If I were not there, perhaps there would be no one to say to them, 'It's okay. You're only human. Nobody's perfect. God loves you anyway.' Yes, I go to church because I love the people there, and I want them to know that they are loved."

"Christian, you're the good shepherd God has led you to be. How can you detest yourself so? Surely you see what good things you do. Surely, if you can see other people, some of whom honestly sin more than you, and say these things, these forgiving things to them, or even of them, to yourself and to me, surely you can see that you are no worse. Surely you can look at yourself and say, 'It's okay. You're only human. Nobody's perfect. God loves you anyway.'"

"I don't know. I suppose it's because the Church is more adamant about condemning my sins than theirs. The Church never sends them letters in the mail, saying, 'Please send money to help battle people like yourself.' The Church never accuses them of trying to destroy it."

"Christian, speak plainly to me. Voice your thoughts. Make them real."

Christian's face was twisted with sorrow. He did not want to discuss it. He was afraid that perhaps Lokiel would just chime in with the Church and say he had to change... even though he could not. It was like asking a fish to breathe on land, or asking a butterfly to be less colorful, these demands the Church had made.

He spoke at last, "Well, as you likely know, I have always been a sort of free spirit. I have always believed in love. I have never believed in repression. I have never encouraged my friends, the people whom I teach in Sunday school, or anyone, to repress themselves. No one should ever hold back from loving someone. But the Church seems to be against me, and they hold up their Bible as evidence that I am beyond salvation.

"I have never repressed my love for anyone, men and women alike. I have never acknowledged that gender line. And why should I? Is beauty not beauty? Is love not love? What's the difference if I love a man or a woman? And today I love a man. I love a man with all of myself, more than myself. So the Church quotes Paul. The Church condemns me to Hell. My friends don't even blink. By all appearances, it doesn't faze them at all, this unnatural way that I live my life. This sweet, illegal love that I know.

"Yet, the skeleton says otherwise. He speaks with such condescending authority. He tells me they hate me just as the Church does. He tells me that none would mourn, were I to end it all right now."

Lokiel's mood had changed. He was now full of fire himself, angry and passionate, no longer lost to sorrow. "Christian, this skeleton is a liar! He is the representative of all that is wrong with the Church! Don't you see it? By what authority does the Church condemn you?"

Christian was moved by the angel's fury, and he took a moment to study him before offering his answer. Lokiel seemed so strong now, and his eyes were fierce, blazing like blue flame in the fire of truth, protective. Christian hated to argue against himself, when this angel seemed so adamant to defend him, but, "Paul. As I said, they quote Paul. They quote the Bible. Surely, if the Bible upon which the church was built says that I am damned, I am."

"No, Christian. Here is the truth. The Church is a good thing, it is a helpful thing, but it is not a perfect thing. The Church can hurt people, the Church can do great wrong, for the Church is as imperfect as its understanding of the Bible upon which its rules are founded, and the Bible is as imperfect as the men who wrote and compiled it."

"But, how can you say that? Are you not the messenger of God?"

"Yes. But I am not the messenger of the Church. I am the messenger of a God who is far older than the Church, far older than Adam, far older than Time. I bring my message from One who sees the Church and her followers for all that they truly are. And I tell you that the Church is flawed."

"But..."

Lokiel pressed on, gently, wanting Christian to understand. Wanting him to accept himself, for this was the only way for Christian to ever defeat the skeleton. "Two men who helped create the Church: Peter and Paul. All one needs to see is a Bible. Peter and Paul were frequently at bitter odds.

They disagreed on so many things, and yet, they are both exalted in the Christian faith. Letters from both are held sacred in the Christian Bible. Letters which show how they could disagree. Don't you see it, Christian? The Church was founded by men who walked with God, yes. They knew the Messiah. However, they could not agree for any sum on the meaning of his words. And that pattern has followed the Church throughout its history, causing divisions, causing wars. It is madness. And as for the issue for which you, by Christ's Church, have been condemned, the great debate that even now threatens to split your denomination in two, Christ himself never uttered a word.

"And would it be so hard to believe, knowing that Christ was God Incarnate, that he was perhaps very much like you? Would it be so hard to believe that, having been the Creator of us all, Christ could see and appreciate the sexual beauty of both male and female? Did God not see what Adam saw when he first knew Eve? Did God not see what Eve saw when she first knew Adam? It is to underestimate the eyes of God to say that He did not. And Christ, being God, surely knew the beauty of both men and women himself. Surely he fell in love with everyone he met. Surely he did."

Christian sat stunned. He could not argue with this wise and passionate angel. "I don't know what to say." He looked guiltily to the gun, still clutched in his hand. Again, he said, "I don't know what to say."

Lokiel studied Christian with affection. "Try, 'I forgive myself.'"

Christian looked up. "I'm not sure."

Lokiel looked sad. "But you need to be." He smiled. "Christian, your friends love you, too. If they didn't, why would they ever see you? Wouldn't it be easy enough to avoid you? That demon skeleton in there is the only reason you think they hate you. He is the reason you were going to end it all. And you must know the truth, it is you who gives him his power. He feeds on your despair. He takes the thoughts that hateful, fearful people have put in your head with their judgments. He takes the twisted words of the Church, and he makes them to wreak havoc in your mind. You must be faithful, Christian. You must accept God's love. Surely, you don't believe that this skeleton is more powerful than God. That jacket is yours. All you need to do is accept it. Open your closet door, and take it, shield yourself from the little remaining winter cold."

Christian began to weep, tears streaming like a river down his cheeks.

Lokiel reached out and laid a hand on the young man's knee. "Christian, why do you weep? Voice your thoughts. Make them real. Why?"

Christian breathed in heavily and sighed. "I weep, because I know it's true. I know you are telling me what is right. I weep, because God loves me, in spite of all that the Church has said. God is beyond the Church, and I believe He loves me, too."

Lokiel, being the sensitive creature that he was, could not help but shed tears with his charge, but still he spoke clearly, "Stand up now, Christian. Go and get your jacket."

Christian looked to Lokiel, and he prayed a silent prayer. A prayer for strength. He stood, and he opened his door.

*   *   *   *

Leaving the door open behind him, leaving Lokiel on the porch, Christian stared at the infernal closet door. He heard remembered words: *The church has rejected you, and therefore so has God...Your soul is a waste...No one really loves you.* He closed his eyes, and he remembered the words of

Lokiel: *As for the issue for which you, by Christ's Church, have been condemned, the great debate that even now threatens to split your denomination in two, Christ Himself never uttered a word...You must accept God's love. Surely you don't believe this skeleton is more powerful than God...Try, 'I forgive myself.'* "I forgive myself." Christian was filled with an electric joy as he realized how truly he had accepted the words of Lokiel. He reached forward and opened the closet door, and his jaw dropped open, and tears once again threatened to blind him. There was his jacket, hanging right before him, beneath a shelf of board games, shoe boxes, and knickknacks, above a vacuum cleaner. There was no skeleton to be seen. God had saved him.

Christian removed his jacket from the hanger, and he put it on, hugging himself and the jacket all at once. He stepped outside in search of Lokiel, but found the porch was empty. He looked away, to the sky, and he saw a winged figure soaring against the sun. The winter breeze hit him then, and Christian smiled, for he was warm at last.

Reverend Philips is Going to Hell

"Though the master loved us all, the shepherd has grown insane and now tends only select members of the flock with the love we all *once knew."*

—The Rainbow-Colored Sheep

1

Reverend Aidan Philips sat alone in his study, looking through a stack of photographs. There were tears in his eyes, both for anger and for sorrow. It was difficult for Reverend Philips to determine whether he had succeeded or failed with young Matthew, as he shuffled the photographs— all of that tragic boy—and thought back to the funeral service he'd presided over just this afternoon. Matthew's funeral. There was a single light turned on in the room. It was the small lamp on the reverend's desk, and it was scarce illumination at best. He stopped shuffling, and he stared at the picture on the top of the stack. It was Matthew's baptism. The day that Matthew had fully renounced his sins and joined Reverend Philips' mission to cleanse the world of evil.

"Oh, Matthew," he spoke with a strain in his voice. "How can you have died so young?" He shook his head. "God had His reasons, of that I am sure. I just don't know what those reasons were. Perhaps you failed to impress Him. Perhaps your penitence came too late. I tried to help you atone for your wickedness. I tried to save you from Hell." Reverend Philips looked intensely at the photograph, as though Matthew himself were attached to it and could hear every word that was said to it. "In the end, I suppose, none of us can hide from our sins. When I found you, the mouth of Hell had already opened at your feet. You were vile and hopeless—damned at the unbelievable age of nineteen. But you followed me, joined my mission, and you fought evil with such vigor that you could have been the very Wrath of God. Perhaps, in the end, the wickedness never truly left your heart. Perhaps God struck you down for it. Perhaps He took you to Hell...and perhaps you deserve Hell."

Aidan Philips pondered his own words in the dark silence. The ticking of the clock and the sound of his breath were his only audible comforts. Three days Matthew had been dead. Three days, and the reverend still couldn't understand it. By all appearances, Matthew had been cured, he had turned on the sinners who'd once been his brethren. He was doing the Lord's work. Even still, God had clearly smote the boy.

The room suddenly took on an unexplained chill, and the reverend placed the photos on the desk and crossed his arms to get warm.

He was startled by the voice of someone else in the room behind him, "And on the third day, he arose from the dead..."

Reverend Philips spun around, "What...?" and found nothing in the darkness. No one to speak these words which he had heard so clearly. "Who's there?" Something drew his eyes to the bookshelves, and as he watched, a figure seemed to pass through the wall beside those dusty shelves—the figure of a man.

As the figure became clearer, the reverend could see that it was smiling at him—warmly. The ghostly figure began to speak, and as it did, it began to look more solid, "...He ascended into Heaven and sitteth at the right hand of God the Father Almighty; from thence he shall come to judge the quick and the dead." It was Matthew. "Isn't that right, Reverend Philips?"

The reverend was clearly terrified. "What demon is this? How is it possible?"

"Actually, the Apostles' Creed isn't *entirely* accurate." The spirit shrugged. "But it really doesn't matter, if we're speaking truthfully. And we are, Reverend Aidan Philips, going to be speaking very truthfully with one another for the remainder of the evening." He grinned. "That's what I'm here for, after all."

The reverend still would not believe his own eyes. Clearly this was a trick of the devil. "Who are you!"

The phantom seemed amused. "Come now, preacher. You know who I am."

Reverend Philips was defiant. "You're not Matthew! Matthew was killed three days ago! His spirit has already been judged and done with!"

The phantom seemed to consider. "Judged, yes. Done with?" He shook his head. "No."

"Lying demon from Hell!" Aidan stumbled to his knees. "I cast you out in the name of Christ!" He lifted a small cross, and he closed his eyes, summoning the strength he associated with his God. "I cast you out in the name of Christ! I cast you out in the name of Christ!"

Feeling playful, the spirit moved silently to stand behind the kneeling preacher.

Slowly opening his eyes to see what the power of God had done to this impostor, Reverend Philips continued his chanting, "I cast you out in the name of..." No phantom. He sighed with relief, "...Christ." He stood then, dusting off his knees. Then he turned.

"Guess what!"

"God Almighty!" The voice and the appearance of the ghost as he turned caused the reverend to flail, collapsing back into his chair.

The phantom now laughed uncontrollably. "No. It's just Matthew!"

Reverend Philips was now more sure than before that this spirit was not his Matthew. So why hadn't God complied and taken the spirit away as he'd prayed? "I will not be mocked by devils. And you must be a devil, because Matthew was never one to play games!"

"Yes," said the spirit, still giggling slightly, "but then I died. And besides, you should have seen the look on your face." The spirit laughed just once more, before his tone went somber. "Laughter is something I forsook in life. Before I met you, I was too determined on self-loathing for laughter. After meeting you, I was, in addition, too determined on hatred of others." He smiled again,

"Let's see how well you know your scripture then. Quote me John, Chapter Eleven, Verse Thirty-Five."

The reverend scoffed at the ease of this challenge, then he answered, "Jesus wept."

"Yes," said the spirit, full of enthusiasm. "And what the Bible fails to mention, though no less true, is this: Jesus laughed."

"Dear God." There was no acceptable explanation for this apparition. "I've lost my mind."

The spirit considered that, as he walked back towards the bookshelves. "Hm. Perhaps you have, but if so, it happened long before tonight, long before my body was destroyed by that drunken bus driver, long before you began your...'mission work.' Yes. If you are mad now, it is only because you've been mad for quite some time. But then, *mad* is such a nasty word. I prefer to think of you as simply misguided." He giggled. "Well, perhaps I should say *complexly* misguided, but misguided, one way or the other, for sure. Either way, it's time to straighten you out. Your 'hour' has come, so to speak."

The spirit pulled a book from the shelf, blowing excessive dust from the cover. "Ah. Dickens. Clever man." He waived the book at the man in the chair and said slyly, "Perhaps you would not be in this predicament tonight, if you would take to heart the books you have read..." He reconsidered, as he shrugged and returned the volume to its place on the dusty shelf, "...or collected anyway."

The preacher still was not hearing a word of it. "What do you want from me? What evil has sent you here to torment me?"

The spirit rolled its eyes with a patient smile. "This is really starting to get old, Reverend Philips. Let me clear this all up, once and for all." He stepped closer to the reverend's chair. "No evil power has sent me here tonight. I am not a demon of any sort. I am Matthew, your one-time follower, who died three days ago. I am sent here by God, because you've gotten yourself into a terrible mess."

Anger tinted the very breath of Reverend Philips, which was not, the phantom noted, an uncommon thing. "What are you trying to say, devil? You can't mean for me to believe that you've been sent here to help me! I'm a minister of God! I'm in no trouble at all! And I'm in no mood for being harassed by one of Satan's supernatural jesters! How dare you offend me like this—whoever you are! My soul is in pain enough! I've just lost a friend, and he was almost a son to me."

"It touches me to hear you say so. All the same, my soul is in pain too, because you were almost a father to me, and you're in such terrible trouble, even as we speak. You see, Reverend Philips, you're going to Hell."

"Lies! I'm an ordained minister of God! I have been baptized in the name of Christ! I have battled evil in the name of the Lord! I have earned my place in God's kingdom!"

"By Man's rules, of course!" the spirit offered. "But God does not bow to Man's rules. The *laws* of Man have so often been the misinterpretation of God's *discretionary* recommendations. God understands so many things that His people can not."

The reverend was unmoved. "You say nothing to convince me!"

The spirit shook its head. "Don't worry, Reverend. The night is so young. I will convince you. You see, the things you have done in God's name have not pleased Him in the least. You call yourself a follower of Christ, but nowhere in the scriptures has Christ done any of the hateful things that you have accomplished. The mission that you have led...the mission that you seduced me into...is a truly evil thing. The people we hurt were people that God loved. The people that we threatened with eternal Hell were people that God favored and understood. They were people that He forgave. Just as God now wishes to forgive you."

"So then, why do you threaten me?"

The spirit answered gladly, pleased that he was at last being heard, "I'm not threatening, I'm warning. Ignorance itself is not a sin, but ignorance by choice is a lethal one. You see, when my body was taken from me on Saturday, I was given a taste of Hell. Not a sentence. Just a taste. What I mean to say is, I was enlightened. I was shown the truth of the things I had done. With that knowledge, I was given back all the pain that I had caused others. The guilt, for a time, was unbearable.

"Then, God enlightened me further. I was given His perspective of myself. I felt God's unconditional love for me. I knew that He understood the circumstances that caused me to follow you. I was confused when you found me. Society and the Church had condemned me, even where God did not. I thought that I was evil, though God saw me only as beautiful. I wanted to change, because the Church said it would please God. You gave me the chance. Though what I did with your ministry was wrong, God understood what had driven me to it. He knew that I was afraid, and confused, and young. He forgave me, and he gave me this opportunity to redeem myself by saving you from yourself.

"God wants you to know that the people you persecute are people you have failed to understand. The people you have most attacked, are the people whom God most wants you to comfort."

The reverend was sickened by the lies of this ghost. "If you really were a messenger from God, you would know that the people I 'attack' are sinners! I give them a taste of Hell so that they will turn themselves away from Satan. I encourage them to change!"

"But, don't you understand, Aidan? They are only sinners by human laws. God doesn't *want* them to change!"

"Then why, as you have said, is it so important to God that *I* change? If God understands these sinners, then why doesn't he understand me?"

The spirit smiled lovingly. "He does understand you. He knows why you are driven by anger, and He is sympathetic. Unfortunately, the fact remains that you have *chosen* hatred. You have *chosen* to ignore the truth of God's mercies. By doing so, you have *chosen* to ignore God. The God in whose name you have persecuted others does not exist, so how can you have a place with the loving God who does exist? If you ignore Him in life, you will ignore Him in death. And God wants you to know Him. He has a new calling for you, but He will not force you to embrace it. You have to choose."

Still unyielding, Reverend Philips was furious. "I have *chosen* a righteous path! And following that path does not include listening to lying devils!"

Frustrated, the spirit let out a sigh. "I see that we will have to do this the hard way, then. If words will not reach you, then perhaps vision will. If vision will not convince you, then surely experience will." He smiled mischievously. "Come now, Reverend Philips! We've got places to go...and you've got people to see."

The spirit lifted a hand and placed it on Reverend Philips' forehead. The shocking cold of the ghostly touch caused the preacher to scream out.

Then, suddenly, everything was very, very dark.

2

In the darkness, Reverend Philips saw nothing, felt nothing. He spoke, "What have you done to me?" And then he could see, but he saw only himself. There was no source of light, and yet he clearly saw what appeared to be his own body, floating in the blackness. There was no sign of the spirit claiming to be Matthew.

"Nothing," came the voice of his deceased disciple. The image of young Matthew then appeared in the blackness as clearly as Reverend

Philips himself. "Well, nothing permanent anyway." He smiled. "I've just taken you out of your body."

The man was afraid. "You've killed me?"

The spirit suppressed a giggle. "No, I've just taken you out of your body. It's okay. I'll put you back." He made a gesture with his right hand. "Scouts' Honor!"

The reverend was confused. "What...what is the meaning of this!"

"I want to show you something. Don't be so freaked out. I thought you'd read Dickens. Don't tell me you were just using that book as a dust magnet. Hm. Have you dusted your Bible lately...Reverend?"

"How dare you imply..." Suddenly, Reverend Philips remembered his surroundings. "Where are we?"

The spirit shrugged. "Nowhere. A void. Don't worry though. This is not where we're headed." He paused to look at the older man thoughtfully. "Tell me, Reverend. Why is divorce wrong?"

Another elementary question. The reverend was irritated. "Divorce is wrong, because it is the breaking of a unity that is made by God. Divorce breaks a promise that is made *to* God."

"I see. And why would someone break such a promise?"

"If you were indeed Matthew, you would know what I had taught you! Marriages are broken by the faithless! Those who divorce do so, because they have no respect for God! They do so, because they are filled with lust for others! They do so, because they are selfish and love only themselves! And such people are doomed to Hell."

The spirit asked simply, "Why?"

"It's in the Bible!" The reverend could stand little more of this demon's ignorance. "The promise of Hell to such sinful people was made by Jesus Christ Himself!"

"No. That's not *even* in the Bible. He never says anything about divorcés going to Hell. He does, however, say, 'What God has united, human beings must not divide.'"

The reverend felt he was making some progress at last with this phantom. "Yes! Even you can't deny it! Jesus condemns any who are divorced!"

"No," said the spirit calmly. "He does not."

Exasperated, the preacher continued to debate, "Why must you be so impossible? How can you argue, when you clearly have no grounds!"

"I have been enlightened. Remember? Let me explain. Over the course of almost two-thousand years, with the myriad translations of an interpretation that began with the twelve dumbest people in the Bible, some of the meanings get lost. It is not divorce that is the sin, but division of the blessed union."

"There is no difference!"

"But there is. Divorce is the *result* of division, because division happens long before divorce. If one spouse abuses another, they become spiritually separated. It is the one who instigates this spiritual separation that is the sinner, and in some cases both of the couple are abusive. If one is abused by a spouse to the point of this spiritual separation, or if one's child is abused by one's spouse, it is arguably sinful to *remain* in that situation, if one has another option."

Reverend Philips would not swallow this spirit's poisonous words. "Blasphemous Hellion! You twist the Word of God!"

"On the contrary, what I am attempting to do for you is to straighten out what has over time become, very truly, the Church's crucified pretzel."

"If you intend to convince me of your obvious lies, you will not do so by insulting the Church!"

"Please, Aidan, don't misunderstand. God loves the Church. He loves it very much. I'm just saying that, like everything of and about Man, the church has its quirks. No one and nothing of this world may claim perfection. Not even if they do so in the name of God. It is still just an arrogant boast. Now, we are here because talking has done us no good, which is why I want you to look for me."

The preacher, once again, felt confused. "Look?"

"Yes."

"What do you mean, 'Look?'"

The spirit, tired of wasting his voice, simply looked ahead, slowly raising his right arm, and pointed. "There," he said simply.

The reverend followed the direction of the spirit's finger, and saw, to his astonishment, a vision, like a planet in the darkness, like a stage. He saw his church, the sanctuary. Himself, Matthew...Sandra. It was the past.

"Do you see?" the spirit asked, with a degree of anger in his voice. He lowered his arm, satisfied that the preacher was with him. "There we are several months ago. With Sandra. The Sunday after she left her husband." He looked to his companion in the void. "Do you remember?"

This vision had given Reverend Philips far more anger than it had given the spirit, but for different reasons. "Yes! That lecherous harlot had broken a most sacred promise to God, and she dared come to us for sympathy." He smiled, smugly. "We let her know that she had offended God. We let her know that she would no longer be welcome in His house."

The spirit argued, "But her husband had put her in the hospital numerous times with his brutality."

"She should have stayed and tried to work things out. It was her responsibility to be a more tolerant wife and to do all in her power to keep from angering her husband, if he was so abusive."

The spirit was clearly sad. "I see." He paused and looked away. He did not want to see what happened here, but he had his task. He resumed, looking again to his companion, "There is a similar scene about to unfold right now. A scene very much like the one that caused Sandra to leave her husband. You are going to be there, but, before we go, look once more into the past. To that Sunday." As they both watched, the spirit's voice became strained by the tears he fought to repress, "Look at Sandra's tears, as she is driven from the church by your screaming voice. Driven away before the entire congregation. Embarrassed. Abandoned. Such a mad, rabid assembly were we. Do her tears not touch you?"

Reverend Philips spoke coldly, sickened by the spirit's own tears and compassion, "They were tears well earned."

The spirit spoke decisively, as he wiped his eyes dry, "We will see."

At that instant, the vision was gone, and so was the void. Suddenly, Reverend Philips found himself surrounded by the clutter of a strange apartment. There was a woman and a man, and this was clearly their living room. The couple was sitting, though not together. The man was drinking beer and watching television. The woman was fidgeting, staring at her hands, not paying attention at all to the program which had captured her husband's eyes.

They didn't appear to see Reverend Philips or the ghost. This puzzled the reverend, until he recalled that he'd been taken out of his body. He himself was like a spirit now. Of course he was invisible to them. Still, he spoke quietly, "Where are we now, monstrosity?"

The spirit answered, "I hope you'll stop insulting me soon, Reverend Philips. I'd hate to have to spank you. We're at the apartment of Jina and Alec Jones. Their son is sleeping just behind that door," he nodded towards a door behind the man's chair, "but it is a fitful sleep. Alec is about to let his wife know that he stumbled across a note from Alec Junior's teacher. It's a note about the boy's attendance."

"So, you think they should be divorced, because they can't get their child to school in the mornings?"

The spirit did not answer. Instead, he said simply, "Shhh. Watch. Listen." And he was silent. Reverend Philips followed suit, when Alec Senior began to speak.

"So," the man said from his chair. "I hear our little ass-wipe is having a problem getting to school."

Jina was horrified. She had not expected Alec to find the note. She answered timidly, trying desperately to think of a sound lie, "Um, yes, well...I..."

He had no patience for her stammering. He took a swig of his beer. "When were you going to tell me about this, Jina?" He stood from his well worn chair. "What the hell do you mean by hiding that note from me? You should have known I'd find it, you stupid bitch!"

Jina stood as well, alarmed by her husband's rising voice. "Alec, you'll wake him."

"Damn right, I'll wake him! I'm his Goddamned father! If you can't get that little shit to go to school with your fuckin' hugs and kisses, I'll beat the little bastard to a bloody pulp and mail 'im there in a shoe box! And I'm fixin' to knock the shit outa' you, too, Goddamnit! Think you're his only fuckin' parent! You don't think I can handle discipline! I can show you better, bitch! I'll discipline the fuck outa' you fat lumps of shit!"

213

Jina was shaking, and she hoped it didn't show. She hoped he was too drunk to put up a real fight tonight. She began walking out of the room. "Alec, please! Can't we talk about this in the morning?" She whispered, "When you're sober."

Alec spun around in a rage to face her. "What? Fuck you! Don't talk under your breath at me! I heard that, you ungrateful bitch! I'm not so drunk I can't knock some sense into you right now!" Striking like lightning, Alec moved forward and slapped his wife with all of his might, sickened by her weakness when she fell to the floor and started sobbing like an infant, curled up in the fetal position.

"Well, Reverend," the spirit broke his silence, "are you still convinced that these two should stay together?"

Reverend Philips gave it some thought. "Yes. She was the perpetuator of this entire situation. She knew her husband was violent, yet she still did something that would assuredly upset him."

"Aren't you curious as to why?"

"No. It's clear. She's weak and selfish."

The spirit now spoke coldly, "I have a gift for you."

Unnerved by the spirit's tone, the reverend asked, "What?"

No answer came. At least, not in words. Reverend Philips felt his consciousness swirl, as if twisted in the winds of a tornado. He lost his bearings completely. Had he gone back to the void? No. There were clearly images. Colors. Pain.

The world stopped spinning. The reverend recognized the feeling of the floor on his side. He was hugging himself. Sobbing. His face hurt. Then it struck him, and he knew what the spirit had done to him. The spirit had taken him from his body and placed him in Jina's. His mind came alive, only to find that it had been replaced. He now thought as Jina did, he remembered all that she remembered, he felt her pain, her protectiveness, her fear. He knew her mind. He knew her heart. He knew what it had been like to live with this man, to try and protect her son and herself. He knew why she had hidden the note. He was Jina now in every way.

He heard Matthew's voice in his head, "Now you're going to *know* the ones you persecute. You're inside of her mind. You have no control, but you will feel all that she feels. You will know all of her thoughts and emotions as she comes to her decision. Don't worry, though. I'm not going to leave you there."

Then came the voice of Alec, and Reverend Philips was afraid, "Get up, bitch! I'm not done with you yet! I'm gonna teach you what happens when you try to hide shit from me! I'll teach you to try and steal my son from me! Get up!"

I have to live, Reverend Philips thought with Jina. *I have to take care of my son.* "Alec, please." She began to rise. "I'm sorry. I'm sorry. I won't do it again! Please, just stop yelling." A foot knocked the reverend down again, and he felt the pain in Jina's chest. The terror in her heart.

"Shut the fuck up! I hate when you whine!" He mocked her, "'Please stop yelling! I'm sorry! I'm sorry!'"

Aidan felt a determination not to whine this time. "Alec. I don't want you to hurt me."

Alec kicked her right in the ribs, and the reverend cried out in pain with her. Alec snarled, "Fuck it! I'm through with you anyway! Now I'm gonna find out why that little shit thinks he's too good to go to school. By God, he will be there tomorrow!"

Reverend Philips sat up with Jina. "Covered in bruises." Jina's son was in danger. All fear was gone. "Why do you think I keep him home so much? Do you want them to take him away from us?"

Alec was beside himself. "You are one nervy bitch tonight!" He bent down, grabbed her by the arms, stood her up and slammed her against the wall by their son's bedroom door. He put his face right up

216

to hers and continued to rail, "Are you calling me a lousy dad? Are you tryin' to tell me it's my fault you can't take his shitty, unwiped, little ass to school? In my experience, eight-year-old, wimpy little kids are not that tough to kick in the ass. And you can kick him in the ass all the way to school! Bitch!" He stood back and slapped her again.

Reverend Philips felt her urge to sob, felt her fight it, wanting to be strong, but then the tears broke through. The pain was too much. She loved this man. She truly loved him. She thought back to their wedding day. How happy she had been. Where did it all go? How could she be receiving this treatment from that man she'd pledged to love. That man she still loved. She knew his gentler side. His weaknesses. His pain. She knew his dreams and how they'd been dashed. She wished that she had been compensation enough. Reverend Philips felt all of this. He loved Alec, as she did, and he was deeply wounded by the treatment she'd been shown. Jina sobbed. The creak of a door caught the reverend's borrowed ear.

"Mommy?"

Aidan felt a great sense of urgency. "Go back to bed, dear. Everything's all right."

Alec Senior disagreed. He turned to see his young, frightened son peeking through his door, opened just a crack. "Come here, you fuckin' little brat! Look what you've done to your damned mommy! I had to beat the shit out of her, because your ass won't go to school. And you know what? You're next, partner. Your right fuckin' now!" He moved to go to his son's room.

"Alec, no." The words were out, before the reverend had even had time to think them.

Alec turned and backhanded her violently. He sneered at her. "Who are you tellin' *no*? I'm teachin' the both of you some manners!" He turned back to his son. "Come'ere you little premature ejaculation!" To Alec's dismay, the boy responded boldly by closing and, by the sound of it, locking his bedroom door. Alec distinctly heard a lock. He stomped over and tried to open it. No luck. Alec was infuriated. He turned again to his wife. "When did you put a fuckin' lock on the kid's door, Jina! What the fuck is wrong with you? Do you think I'm a monster? Is that it? Do you think I'm a drunk?" This time, slapping wasn't good enough. Alec made a fist and punched Jina in the face with all of his rage.

Reverend Philips saw stars, he felt pain in Jina's head, but he didn't black out. He couldn't black out. He had to stop Alec from hurting their son. The taste of blood overpowered him, and something hard was in his mouth. He felt Jina spit out a tooth. They regained their balance. They had to.

Alec went to his son's door and shouted at the top of his drunken lungs, "I hope you don't think that lock is stronger than me, sport! You and your mommy are about to wish you never conspired against me!" He began kicking at the door, harder and harder.

Reverend Philips found himself looking frantically all over the room, seeking a solution. Suddenly, Jina's eyes fixed on a half empty beer bottle. She rose and went to it, clutching it. Alec was so intent on breaking down his son's door that he never even noticed. Reverend Philips moved up behind Alec then and, with Jina's sense of urgency, broke the bottle over the drunken man's head.

Alec turned dizzily. "What the fu..." He never finished his question.

Reverend Philips knew, as Jina knew, that her husband must not be allowed to recover. Thinking only of the safety of the little boy in the next room, Reverend Philips, still holding the broken bottle in Jina's shaking hand, thrust the jagged glass right through Alec's chest. Alec gave his wife a look of disbelief, then he fell to the floor, landing with a crunch on the bottle, which protruded from his chest. Still needing to be sure, Reverend Philips proceeded to break two more bottles over

Alec's bleeding head. He then broke the child's door down himself.

"No!" came the frightened eight-year-old's cry.

"It's okay, sweetie," Reverend Philips assured him. "It's Mommy. Close your eyes, honey. Everything's going to be all right." Aidan entered the child's room and scooped him up in Jina's arms. Tears were streaming down both their faces, as the reverend covered the boy's eyes with Jina's protective hand and carried him out of the room. "We're just going to let Daddy sleep for a while."

Then, suddenly, everything was very, very dark.

3

A voice came out of the darkness, "Well, how are you feeling?" And Reverend Philips saw the form of Matthew.

The older man felt tears flowing easily from his eyes, and he too became visible in the void. "How could I have known she loved him so? How could I have known that she was so brave? You were right about the separation. Oh...Matthew, you were right. He was not her husband, and that was no fault of hers. She tried to hold things together. She hid that note, because she knew he would beat their son if he knew about it. She was willing to take that beating in her son's place. But now, she has nowhere to go. He was her support. He's probably dead. What is she going to do?" The reverend struggled, trying to articulate his strange feelings. "I can't put it into words. How much she loves her son. How much she even loves her husband!" Anger returned to the man's voice, "He's a monster! He's the one who belongs in Hell!"

Matthew shook his head with a tired smile. "No. You're coming along, and our journey goes well, but we aren't there yet. God does not make monsters. And, as you soon will see, nothing that God creates is any sort of abomination. Just as God knows your story, and is willing to forgive you, just as he knows my story and Jina's story, God knows Alec's story. God knows better than Alec what circumstances led to the way he lived. If there is cause for Alec to be pitied and forgiven, it is known only to God. That is why it is only for God to judge us; for only God can judge us fairly. You can't worry about the splinter in Alec's eye, when there still remains this great log in your own. 'Take the log out of your own eye first, and then you will see clearly enough to take the splinter out of your brother's eye.'"

Reverend Philips considered it. Scripture stood clearly against him. He shook his head woefully. "I've been so wicked." He looked to his guide. "Take me home, Matthew, and I'll be a better man."

"No. I'm afraid we're not yet finished."

"Surely I've not transgressed anymore!" Reverend Philips didn't understand. "I understand now what you were telling me, Matthew. I don't need anymore lessons."

Matthew looked bothered. "I want to believe you, but I'm afraid I can't."

"Why not?"

"Look." Matthew pointed again, as he gazed into the distance. "It's the past again."

The reverend took in the vision, as it came into focus. "Our mission trip!"

Matthew spoke through a pain in his ghostly heart, "Four days ago."

Reverend Philips was overcome with zeal. "Such a glorious way for your ministry with me to end. You fought evil like the very wrath of God!" He looked to his former disciple. "In my eyes," he said proudly, "you proved that you had defeated your own wickedness."

Matthew was outraged, as he looked at his former self, the reverend, and all of the others, standing in that alley with baseball bats...waiting. "No! I tormented the innocent, and I defeated only

223

myself. In life, I was so confused, but now I understand. God does not create abominations. Everything is created with a wonderful purpose."

Reverend Philips could not believe his ears. Had Matthew truly learned nothing from him? "They were all perverts! Look at them! Men holding hands with men! Men kissing men!"

Matthew watched the vision of the past, as they prepared to put their bats to deadly use...all in the name of the god of love, and he could not help but weep. "It's only as perverted as men and women doing the same things. There is no sin in mutual affection. Truly, there are only two sexual sins: sexual acts with one who does not consent and sexual acts with one who does not understand. These are, however, forgivable sins, just as all sins are, and failure to forgive a sin is in itself a sin. But even that is an understandable and forgivable sin. God is love; therefore, why would God be offended at anyone for sharing love?"

The reverend would hear none of it. "No! It is specified in the Bible that homosexuality is a sin! Punishable by death! Look at Sodom and Gomorrah! Obliterated."

Matthew would not be ignored. "The sin of Sodom and Gomorrah was not homosexuality, but inhospitality and rape. It was customary then to invite strangers into your home and protect them from the harsh desert night. Only Lot was good enough to invite the visiting angels inside. Then, the men of the town, who had refused the angels hospitality, commanded Lot to release the angels so that the men could rape them. Surely you can see that these crimes would have been just as horrible if the angels had been women. Homosexuality wasn't the real issue. If you believe the Bible was so adamantly against homosexuality, perhaps you should take a closer look at David and Jonathan. That sort of relationship was commonplace among soldiers of the time."

Reverend Philips was disgusted. "If God had wanted men to lay with men, he wouldn't have given Adam an Eve. Homosexuality is a sin, because it goes against God's command to be fruitful and multiply! Homosexuals insult God with their disregard for His plan! They are sick! They are abominations! That was the whole idea behind our mission trips! We reminded them of Sodom and Gomorrah! We proved to them that God's wrath will rain down on them for their evil ways! God really doesn't even need us! Why do you think He sent them AIDS!"

Matthew was in a silent rage of his own. He could hardly tolerate his former mentor's raving ignorance; however, it *was* ignorance, and it needed to be corrected. "If we're going to be rational here, I should point out to you that AIDS is now most commonly found in heterosexual women. Not in homosexual men *or* homosexual women. That fact alone is very strong evidence that AIDS is not a punishment for homosexuality."

Deaf to all reason, Reverend Philips watched the vision of the past with excitement. "Look! Look at the way they are! They rebel against nature! Look, there's our group!"

Matthew fought the urge to turn away, but he knew he must face it all again, for these had been his sins as well. "Oh, God. I can scarcely stand to watch! Please." He saw what he'd dreaded. "Oh, there I am. There we go, attacking with baseball bats and clubs. Screaming inaccurate scripture at the top of our lungs. I almost lost it when I faced Jeremy again. You know, he had been my lover, before you 'rescued' me from my own wickedness during your previous mission trip. I didn't think I had it in me." He looked on, watching himself through blurred vision. Watching himself murder the innocent. "So, when I managed to bring that bat down on his skull, and then...go on quoting scripture as though nothing was wrong, I thought I had saved myself from the past. In truth, it was completely the opposite. *I* was the one rebelling against nature. I was fighting my own nature, as God had created it. As God had intended it." He looked into the older man's eyes. "Do their screams of injustice not move you? Do their screams of pain not stab at your heart like a spear?"

Reverend Philips could see, in those teary, phantom eyes, that Matthew already knew the answer and meant to correct him harshly. He thought of his experience from a few moments before, when he'd *become* the very sort of woman he'd once persecuted. He was chilled at the thought of what Matthew might do to him now. He spoke with a quiver in his voice, "Matthew, please don't do this to me."

Matthew looked at him sternly, not even the hint of a smile on his lips, and he said flatly, "You have to understand them."

Just as had happened before, Reverend Philips was surprised by the sudden vanishing of both vision and void. He was in a restaurant then with Matthew, the pair of them facing a small table, where two men sat chatting. Panic took its grip on the reverend. "Please don't do this, Matthew. I can't bear it! I'll die if you make me do this!"

The phantom made no acknowledgement of his companion's pleading. "Michael and Brad are both gay, but they themselves are not a couple in that fashion. They've been best friends now for three years."

Hopefully, the reverend asked, "Matthew, if they're just friends, then what is it you want to show me?"

Matthew answered quietly, with a finger to his ghostly lips, "Shhh. Watch. Listen."

Michael was laughing, but he wound it down and spoke to the matter at hand, "So, anyway, Brad, enough chit-chat. What is it that you wanted to talk to me about?"

Brad looked back and forth nervously, avoiding Michael's eyes. "Um, what do you mean?"

Knowing Brad as he did, Michael could tell the other man was feigning ignorance. "You sounded upset on the phone earlier, when you asked me to meet you here." Michael grinned smugly. "I've known you long enough to pick up on all your subtle nuances, buddy. What's up?"

Brad let out a long breath, conceding that he'd lost all the confidence he'd had when he'd made that phone call. "I shouldn't have called you."

"Why? What's going on?"

"Nothing. Just forget it."

"Brad, you're really starting to scare me. What is it?"

Brad forced a smile, trying to play it off. "I'm sorry. It's nothing, really. I'm sorry I bothered you. Let's just go on talking as if I *hadn't* had an urgent tone in my voice when I called you."

Michael was almost angry at this. "No. Brad, you've said enough of nothing to keep me up for nights with worry. Now, tell me what is going on with you, or I promise to be pissed off forever." He smiled, but Brad continued to frown. "Hey, you were supposed to laugh at that, not frown. What's wrong? You look so damned brooding!"

Again, the other man sighed. "I can't stand to have you mad at me." He looked his worried friend in the eyes. "I'll tell you, but only if you promise that we'll still be friends afterwards. No matter what I say."

Agitated, Michael agreed, "Of course. Shit. You're scaring me to death. What is it?"

Brad was still unsure. "First, picture the worst thing I could possibly say. Something that would absolutely destroy our friendship."

"God damn it, Brad! Just spit it the hell out, will you!"

Very tensely, Brad looked down at the table. "All right. Hoo, this is not easy for me to say."

Michael laughed affectionately. "Obviously. I've never seen you like this." He met Brad's troubled eyes and smiled. "Go on."

Another sigh, and, "Well, last night...oh, I can't believe I'm telling you this."

"Brad!"

"All right, all right. You see, last night, when we were out with everybody...oh, boy." He fidgeted. "Well, the thing is...that...when I saw you and David all off alone in the corner, and I saw how happy you looked together, I...I wanted to punch his lights out!"

Michael was shocked. He thought he knew where this was headed, but he asked anyway, his voice weakened to just above a whisper, "Why?"

Brad realized there was no going back at this point, and this made it much easier to keep going forward. He looked Michael directly in the eyes, hoping he would find understanding there, as he spoke passionately, "Because I was jealous. Because, I'm not comfortable with us just being friends anymore. It's just that...you're the best friend I've ever had, and I didn't want to, but I've obviously fallen in...oh, I'm so stupid!" Brad put his face in his hands and looked as though he would tear it apart. "I'm sorry, Michael. I can't believe I said that!" He looked up, tears in his eyes, not meeting Michael's gaze. An angry scowl crossed his face, and he slammed a fist down onto the table, just before he stood abruptly and ran outside.

Michael sat, stunned, looking at the spot where Brad had been sitting.

Reverend Philips had been watching the scene unfold with disgust. Matthew turned to him.

"Now, Reverend Philips, I have another gift for you."

The reverend was terrified. "Oh, Matthew, please don't." It struck him then, swirling reality, then colors, images...sorrow.

Now in Brad's body, shaken by despair, Reverend Philips put a cigarette to his lips and smoked nervously. So many thoughts were forcing themselves onto the reverend's consciousness. Thoughts of Michael, how happy he made him feel, how good he was, how wonderful it would be to be his partner and build a life with him. How badly he had screwed up their friendship. How he would rather die than go on without Michael's affection.

The door beside him opened, and Michael joined him in the cold winter night. As Brad, Reverend Philips felt himself tense up. He didn't want to look at Michael, but he forced himself. He had to fix this. He turned to face Michael's smiling face. The smile meant there was hope for salvaging their friendship. "Look," he said. "I understand if you don't want to be friends anymore. I know I should have just left it alone." He almost cried, and the pain was almost too much for Reverend Philips to take, when he said, "Nothing has to change between us...but...I just can't handle us not being friends at all." It was

231

agony, looking into Michael's beautiful face, a face that left him unable to question the existence of God, as he waited for his reply, intensely attracted, braced for the utter decimation of his yearning heart.

Michael spoke at last, still grinning, as though he were amused by the whole thing. "Brad, I want you to know something."

Reverend Philips felt the hurt with Brad, his thoughts raced through Brad's past, the history of rejection, one after another, the rejection of friends and family, the rejection of girls who'd loved him, the rejection of everyone who'd ever failed to understand him. All he wanted was this one thing. All he needed in the world was for this one person to love him as intensely as he himself loved. Now, he feared he was going to be let down easy. Rejected again. He thought his heart would stop beating at any moment. He thought he would die. He looked away from Michael and asked the ground, "What?"

Michael spoke with a sureness that made Brad nervous, "I want you to know what I was thinking, when I was talking with David last night."

The reverend felt Brad's agony. Together, they thought, *Why must he tell me this? Why must he put me through this? Why doesn't he just get it over with?*

Michael continued, "You see, I was thinking about how he had a very nice smile, and he had a lot of interesting things to say, and there was a certain twinkle to his eyes. I was thinking about what nice company he was."

Reverend Philips felt queasiness in Brad's stomach and feared he was about to throw up. This was sadistic. Perhaps Michael was torturing him as revenge for destroying their friendship. Thoughts of agony assaulted him, threatened to overwhelm him. He thought of losing Michael, how he would not want to live, because he compared everyone to Michael, and now he would never love again.

But Michael hadn't finished yet, and Brad was too upset to stop him, when he said, "But I wasn't very good company myself. I was distracted, because I was wondering where you had gotten off to. I was comparing him to you in every way and thinking that I'd rather be talking to you."

Hope filled the reverend, as it filled Brad's heart. *Could it be?*

"You see," Michael went on, "I have a habit of comparing everyone I meet to you. I couldn't help but think that his smile was nowhere near as nice as yours, his conversation was nowhere near as interesting, and the twinkle in his eyes

233

didn't even come close to exciting me the way that your sparkling eyes do."

He's moving closer, the reverend realized with Brad. *The way he's looking at me...Is this really happening? If this is a trick, I'll die right here.*

Michael stood so close to Brad, that Brad could feel his breath as he spoke, "Brad, I fall asleep every night with your name on my silent lips." He paused, then his voice began to quiver, "I've been in love with you for longer than I can recall. You're the best friend I've ever had, and I was always afraid to jeopardize that friendship, because you might not feel the same." Michael was clearly fighting back tears. "I'm so glad you found the courage to tell me how you feel."

He lifted a hand, and he caressed Brad's face tenderly. The feeling sent electricity through every atom of Brad's being, and Reverend Philips thought he would burst with joy, when Michael said, "You're the only one I want. You're my knight in shining armor, and I want you by my side forever."

Reverend Philips felt Brad bubbling over, unable to hold back anymore. "Michael, oh, God. This is like a fairy tale. This is like a dream, and I pray God I never wake up."

Michael moved in closer still, caressing the back of Brad's head, running fingers through his hair.

"Well, I don't know about you, but I feel like making up for lost time, and let's not lose any more."

There were so many words in Brad's head, and Reverend Philips felt the confusion, the uncertainty of which words to say. It all came out in one, "Okay." Michael's face touched his then, and his lips met Brad's in a tender kiss. It was the sweetest kiss from the truest love that Reverend Philips had ever experienced, and he never wanted it to end.

Then, suddenly, everything was very, very dark.

4

Reverend Philips' voice pierced through the darkness, "Matthew. Thank you." His image became clear. He felt so humbled, so ashamed. So deeply, deeply ashamed.

"Thank God. Not me." Matthew became visible in the void, and he smiled. "How do you feel?"

"Refreshed. Yes, as fresh as young love." He looked to Matthew sadly. "How could I have misunderstood so completely? Oh, Matthew, their love for each other was so pure! There was nothing wicked or sinful about it. In fact, now the only truth I see is that it would be a sin for them *not* to be together. I know now, as I once loved my wife, as I still love my wife, even in her absence, so does Brad love Michael. And I want them to have each other, just as I want my own beloved to return to me. But, as you show me who I truly am, I begin to forget why I blamed her for going."

Matthew spoke with understanding, "You never granted her a divorce."

"It would have been a sin." The words seemed suddenly alien to Aidan Philips.

"A sin?"

The reverend conceded, "I wanted her to stay. I wanted to have my way. I caused a rift in our marriage...with my hate. She had no stomach for it, and now, neither do I."

Matthew put a hand on the reverend's shoulder. "After tonight, you'll have the rest of your life to make amends, if you choose. And I hope you will, as I can not. My time's been spent, and how precious time seems when it's gone. Only the dead can know." He paused. "There is one more lesson for you tonight, and then, I think, you're done."

Reverend Philips pleaded, "Matthew, what more could there be! I know I've been terrible. I know it! I will make amends."

"My friend, you've come so far tonight. I assure you, I believe you're saved. However, we must be sure. There is still another heinous crime, which we must face. And it is very similar to the last one. So, I ask you, is an interracial child an abomination, in God's eyes? Would you dare to dig up some scripture and tell me that it is? I am curious, now that you have seen so much truth, can you still cling to your hatred of anyone?"

"Matthew...it's hard for me. I am sure of what you're about to show me, and I am sure that I detest myself for it. I can't argue with you, but, I must confess, the thought of interracial unions leaves me sick. I know it's not right to say so, but it is truth. I know now, rationally, these children are not abominations, but emotionally, the sight of them makes me angry. And now, my anger makes me ashamed. I want to ask you not to do this...not to make me watch this, but...I know this for a gift now. I cherish it."

"I am glad, and we'll not stay long now, for the lesson of love to be learned is little different than the lesson just learned. However, the crime is vastly different. Look. There we are...exhuming the body, your disciples fighting off the parents. Mr. and Mrs. Cole. The black father and white mother of the dearly departed Joseph Cole, five years old. Need I remind you?"

Reverend Philips averted his eyes from the vision of the past. "No. We...didn't know. The father never came to church, so we didn't know until after the funeral. The child looked white. But when we learned that the black man at Cynthia's side was the father...we dug the child up and removed the body from our burial ground. It was unclean." Reverend Philips truly knew he'd been wrong. He already felt the dread regret that would now be with him all his life. "I was so horrible to those grieving parents. I told them that their son...was in Hell. And now I'm bound for Hell." He looked at Matthew, tears in his eyes. "I want to go now."

"Home?"

"No." The preacher looked back to the horrific vision. "I want to feel this. I want to be this, so that I will never forget. So that, instead of my revulsion, I will remember their love."

The vision was gone, as was the void. It was a child's bedroom that now surrounded them, and there was a little girl in bed. A little girl who was clearly of mixed ancestry, and she was folding her hands, ready to pray. Beside her was a white man, who held the hand of a black woman, as they knelt beside their daughter's bed, to guide her through her prayers.

Matthew spoke, "Go, now, Reverend Philips. Learn what you must learn."

There was no fighting it this time, and Reverend Philips was easily the little girl, without any disorientation. He felt her love of God, her six-year-old's awe at the concept of the Almighty, as he uttered with her the child's prayer, "Now I lay me down to sleep..." He felt her security in the company of her parents, thought back on loving things they'd said, how she'd brought a drawing home from school of a purple duck with nine legs, and they'd told her how wonderful it was and hung it on the refrigerator.

He became the mother. He felt her protectiveness. How she didn't want to see anything ever hurt her baby. But he also felt her jaded faith. He remembered how she'd gone to church a month ago with her family, how no one would speak to them, but people freely stared. How she'd decided that church wasn't good enough for her baby girl. That if God wouldn't accept her, then she wouldn't let God near her. Except here, where she could keep an eye on things. Here, where no one could stare.

Then he was the father, so in love with his family, rewarded by their love in kind. He looked at his daughter as she prayed, and he was filled with pride. He looked over to his wife, and she met his eyes, knowing, loving. How this man loved his wife! He would do anything for her, and he would do anything for their daughter. He was still determined to bring her up in the Church, but he was slowly losing hope that they would ever be accepted. The love that Reverend Philips felt in this couple was as bright as the love he felt for his own estranged wife. It was as bright as the love that Brad felt for Michael. And brighter still was the love they both felt for their daughter, and the love their daughter felt for them. Reverend Philips wanted to stay in the room, a spirit, passing from mind to mind and feeling this love.

And then, suddenly, everything was very, very bright.

5

At least, it seemed bright compared to the void he'd been expecting to return to. But this was no void. This was Reverend Philips' study, where he'd first encountered the spirit of Matthew. He'd been so different then. He was sitting in the very chair he'd been in before he'd left. Or had he left? He was confused. What a vision he'd been given. But what was he to do with it? "I've been so horrible," he said aloud. He wept. "All those people that I hurt."

He felt a hand on his shoulder, and Matthew's gentle voice, "Aidan."

"Matthew. I have offended God as no man ever has. Every life that I have touched is far worse for it. I have earned Hell. You're right. I belong in Hell as none have ever belonged there before."

Matthew smiled and came around to face him, kneeling. "No, Aidan, you don't. Use this experience, and the opposite is true. You belong here as few before you have. God has given you a gift tonight. It is the gift of understanding. The gift of enlightenment. Of course, enlightenment could just as easily have damned you, had it not changed your heart. In fact, the only reason you were in danger of Hell at all was that I had come to show you your true self and give you this curse of enlightenment, and the opportunity to turn it into a gift. Had you chosen to ignore this experience, you would have chosen to continue ignoring God Himself. But having chosen to embrace it, you now have the rest of your life to use it. You have a new calling, as I said before."

"Please, Matthew, what is this calling...exactly?"

Matthew stood and smiled down at his friend. "The Church builds walls, where they should have built doorways. You, in times past, have been a great builder of walls. Now, you'll knock them down. The Church believes that all their sheep

243

must be alike, all with pure white fleece. This is not the case. God loves the sheep whose fleece is multi-colored just as well. The rainbow-colored sheep. This is to be your ministry, Reverend Philips. These people who we visited tonight are God's rainbow-colored sheep, rejected by the Church, mistaking that rejection for God's rejection. I would have shown you so much more, if we'd had the time tonight. I would have shown you a man named Anthony, one of God's lost sheep, who years ago felt rejected by the Church. He tried to hide his multi-colored fleece, but was eventually disenchanted and, just over six years ago, was seduced to his detriment by one of the wolves who wait to snatch such people up as soon as they turn from God. I would have shown you a man named Christian, who was in a similar spot, ready to kill himself only a year ago. I would have shown you his strength now. How he listened to the messenger of God and learned to let go of the lies the Church can tell in God's name. I would have shown you so many of the rainbow-colored sheep, like Jina and her family, Brad and Michael, and the family we only just left, so that you would know your flock. But, as it is, they will come to you, and you must embrace them. These people want to know that God loves them, and you are called to witness this truth, that God does love them, as you do.

"So, your new calling, until the day we meet again, is to be a shepherd to all those you've turned away, and their like. Judge no one. Nurture and minister to the very same people you have persecuted in the past. Defend them. Let them know that God loves them and understands them as no human institution can."

"Yes, but, Matthew, how do I begin?"

Matthew started to walk towards the wall he'd first passed through that evening. "Opportunity will knock, as they say. Just open the door." Matthew offered one last smile, as he vanished through the wall.

Reverend Philips sat for a moment, pondering all that he had witnessed. Then he was startled by a knocking on his front door. The reverend made his way to answer the door and opened it to find Jina and her son. The very same Jina whom he'd been through so much with that very night. "Dear God!"

She spoke hoarsely, as she held her son to her shoulder. "Forgive me, sir, for troubling you so late, but...a young man on the street sent me to this address. He said you were a good, kind man." She looked so frightened, and yet so hopeful. "He said that you would help me."

Reverend Philips took in the sight of her, the bruises, the dried blood on her shirt, her eyelashes heavy with the wetness of tears. He knew that he was truly being blessed. "Come in, please. I'll get you anything you need. I have a guest room, if you need a place to stay."

Jina seemed at a loss for words. She hadn't even told this man what she'd been through, but she felt he knew somehow. "I...don't mean to be such a burden."

"Nonsense." He smiled warmly. "I'm a minister of God. You can tell me everything, and I'll help you in every way I can." He ushered them inside, and as he closed the door behind them he said, "There's no inconvenience." Then he whispered, mostly to himself, "You're here to save me too."

www.ingramcontent.com/pod-product-compliance
Lightning Source LLC
Chambersburg PA
CBHW051724260326
41914CB00031B/1725/J